About the Author

Born in London 1931, Frank was evacuated, for a short time, at the outbreak of the Second World War. Back home, Frank went through some bombing raids; in particular, the 'Doodlebugs', the flying bomb and, later, the more threatening V2 rockets.

At eighteen years of age, he was conscripted to two years' army service.

He later joined the Merchant Navy in 1957, travelling the world in a tramp steamer.

Frank emigrated to Australia in 1960, where he worked on major dam and road projects and as a kangaroo shooter in the outback, New South Wales. He met his first wife, and with three children to support, got a permanent job with NSW railways.

Snapshots

Frank M. Kelly

Snapshots

Olympia Publishers
London

www.olympiapublishers.com
OLYMPIA PAPERBACK EDITION

Copyright © Frank M. Kelly 2020

The right of Frank M. Kelly to be identified as author of
this work has been asserted in accordance with sections 77 and 78
of the Copyright, Designs and Patents Act 1988.

All Rights Reserved

No reproduction, copy or transmission of this publication
may be made without written permission.
No paragraph of this publication may be reproduced,
copied or transmitted save with the written permission of the
publisher, or in accordance with the provisions
of the Copyright Act 1956 (as amended).

Any person who commits any unauthorised act in relation to
this publication may be liable to criminal
prosecution and civil claims for damage.

A CIP catalogue record for this title is
available from the British Library.

ISBN: 978-1-78830-560-0

First Published in 2020

Olympia Publishers
Tallis House
2 Tallis Street
London
EC4Y 0AB

Printed in Great Britain

Contents

THE EARLY RECOLLECTIONS 9
PRE-1930..11
FROM 1930 ONWARDS..14
THE TOT'S VIEW OF THE WORLD 19
BICYCLE FAMILY 34
HULLBRIDGE..40
WAR TALK...43
MOVE TO CANNINGTON ROAD 45
WOOLAVINGTON...48
BACK HOME..63
THE WAR CONTINUES 65
SOUVENIER HUNTING 70
TEIGNMOUTH..76
BIFRONS 84
MATCHSTICK ISLAND AND THE DOODLEBUGS..90
THE HAIRY GANG..93
THE CREEPING-IN-SHOP......................................98
STREET URCHINS...101
DAY AT THE ZOO...106
PULLING A SWIFTIE..108
THE V2s TO THE END OF THE EUROPEAN WAR.110

LIFE IN THE BUTCHERS SHOP	115
AUSTERE BRITAIN	119
GRIMY LONDON	138
HAINS AND WARWICK	142
EPILOGUE	147

THE EARLY RECOLLECTIONS

This collection of early memories is mainly a chronicle of events that perhaps a future family member, or a curious person, might find interesting and may wish to gain an insight into the way of life, the feelings and the struggles of a family member in the 1930s and 40s. It may only be a depiction of the life of a working-class family living on the outskirts of London, but it was a life played out in many families of that era: a way of life that will never be repeated.

Possibly, it might be interesting for others researching events of Dagenham in that period. It is not a complete history, merely the feeble recollections of one person 60 to 70 years after the events. Obviously, some events have been forgotten and the episodes not in strict chronological order. One child's memories, or believed perception of events, will not be quite the same as another's, even in the same family; for example, my brother Dennis and I were born only 13 months apart, and in the early years, at least until the mid-war years of 1941-42, did practically everything together. I am sure though that his early recollections of what we did together would differ somewhat from mine. Carrying the comparison further, a child reared in a city would perhaps place a different emphasis to particular events compared to someone born in the country. Perhaps most events shaping happy memories occur during fine sunny weather when one tends to be happier, whereas with dismal weather the more unpleasant memories are suppressed, dependent of course to their importance in shaping one's future. That brings us to the main reason I have put these memories down, which is: if it is not done, it all will be forgotten. I again emphasise these are only my recollection of events and how they affected me. If any of the surviving members of our family group want to add to this chronicle, perhaps they could add an appendix or small anecdote.

PRE-1930

The Great Depression that started with the Wall Street Crash in 1929, and spread throughout the western world, caused huge unemployment, hardship and immense social disruption. It seemed to be the turning point from the ideals and expectations of the twenties to the reality of real social changes taking place around the world; Britain was no exception. By August 1930, the number of unemployed in Britain had reached 2 million; increased social unrest; rioting in several cities; and instances of pitched battles fought between the police and unemployed occurred in various places around the country. Father related to us of a particularly violent, ugly fight that took place between unionists and the police in Trafalgar Square, London, where many were injured. In those days, the government had no hesitation in using force to break up striker's meetings with baton-wielding police on horseback.

Where work was available, the employer had the upper hand. Many a tale our father used to tell of lining up daily in a queue at one of the London Docks, while the boss would walk along the line picking out the men he thought most able. Some of the work was extremely heavy, laboriously unloading ships or barges laden with bricks or bags of flour or whatever.

These years of hardship on top of the 1914-18 war – the bloodiest yet fought between European countries – and which was optimistically called 'The war to end all wars', went a long way in determining the mindset of men from that era. In particular, working-class men, some of whom looked with interest and admiration at the alleged successes of the new Soviet Union depicted by communist propaganda as a working-class man's utopia. Many thought their sacrifices in the war had been in vain and only for the benefit of the privileged and well off.

In October of 1929, our parents, with Henry, aged eight; Mildred, aged six; and Pat, aged three, in tow, immigrated to Canada. Details of their reasons for emigrating at that time, with such huge unemployment worldwide and just before Canada's always predictable severe winters set in, were never explained to us; perhaps it was the hope that better employment opportunities would be available there. However, the result was a disaster, in the fact that our father could not obtain permanent employment over there, and in late 1930 or early 1931, they returned to England disappointed. It was always with bitterness that he talked to us about the Canadian experience. To make matters worse, they returned to an England still in the throes of the Depression. Unemployment in the early 1930s was still high in England, as in the whole industrial world; for instance, in the USA it was over 11 million.

Our parents on the deck of the immigrant ship, 'Princess of Atholl' 1929. Dad standing at the back, holding Pat. Mum on his right, behind Henry who is wearing a school cap; Mildred is on Henry's left.

FROM 1930 ONWARDS

Life must have been extremely tough for the family at the time. Another child was born in January 1930, Edwin Sidney, when they were still in Canada. Unfortunately, he died from meningitis shortly after arrival back in England.

When I was born, we lived in a shared house in Devons Road, Bow, and a favourite tale later was how because they never had a cot for me, they used a drawer from the cupboard to lay me in. The family moved to Dagenham in the early 1930s, during one of the great East London slum clearance projects. This clearance began in the late 1920s. London, forever growing and spreading, was again at bursting point and the crowded East End where housing was of poor quality, was at saturation point, and there lived most of the poor people and new immigrants.

I was born in Poplar Hospital, near Bow, on 25th November 1931. The Kelly family that arrived in Davington Road, Dagenham, (a family of six) sometime in 1932/33 consisted of, in addition to myself; Father, Henry Fredrick Kelly, born 1899; Mother, Florence Merna Kelly, born 1901; their eldest son was Henry, born 1921; their daughter, Mildred, was born 1923 and another son, Patrick, was born 1927. Unfortunately, another son, Edwin Sidney, born 1930, died before the family moved to Dagenham. Dennis was born in Stepney, December 1932; then youngest son, Edwin Stanley was born in 1935, in Upney Hospital, 1935.

Our branch of the Kelly family was long established in England; in fact, earlier generations had a strong association with the British army.

Our grandfather, Thomas Edwin Kelly, was a councillor for Poplar Council. Sometime in the 1920s, he along with fellow councillor George Lansbury, got into trouble with the authorities over some contentious annual levy, which they both thought unjust, resulting them being sent to Brixton jail for 'contempt of court'. After public outrage, they were released, and later the law was changed.

Personally, I can only recall seeing him a couple of times, and my vague memory of him was of a grumpy old man, but that perhaps was the perception of a very young child looking at an old man. Maybe the grumpiness was directed at my father. We saw more of our grandmother later, after grandfather died. Of our mother's family, we only ever saw her brother, Uncle Harry. She never volunteered any information on her family.

One can imagine the difficulties of rearing a family of six children on the sole income of a council worker. In these days of easy birth control, it is easy to say why did they have so many children and why didn't they stop after the fourth one died. Large families were the norm in pre-war days, so it couldn't have been easy to avoid. I suppose you would have to put yourself in their shoes to understand that contraception in those days was largely unreliable. One fortunate thing for us about them not stopping there is that, if they had, Dennis,

Edwin and myself would have not been born, and then our memories would have been someone else's.

I don't know the details of how word of the availability of re-housing in Dagenham got about, but I know it was a saviour for our family, and who knows how our lives would have turned out if we didn't move. Though later in life we (the children) used to complain about the housing estate, and the lack of facilities for youth, for the young parents in the early 1930s it was like a new start in life and certainly better for our future than in the slums of London.

For our father, the chance of a new house in the great housing project of Dagenham, and the prospect of a permanent job working for the local council, was too good an offer to miss. The hundreds of new houses being built augured well for future on-going maintenance, so full time work was virtually assured.

The first house we moved into was a terraced house in Davington Road on the Becontree estate; the house was large by Bow standards, but very small compared to present day expectations, and was reasonably close to the shops at the Round House and the Robin Hood. As with all houses on the estate, it had a back garden and a small front garden with a privet hedge fronting the street. Washing was done by boiling the clothes in a copper; the clothes were then put through the hand wringer. Many a child lost a finger or two in the gears of the wringer, a constant worry for the parents. Dad had a finger missing through a wringer mishap, and used to entertain us in the early days by pretending his finger was right up his nose and other such type of tricks.

Dad was a keen gardener and soon had a garden growing with a trellis for the roses and a concrete path to the clothesline.

The Ford Motor works was the largest employer in Dagenham; in England the name Dagenham became synonymous with the Ford Motor works. It had its own docks and was served well by railway shunting yards; no wonder it received more than its share of air attacks during the war.

I can't say our financial situation was worse than it was for others in that era, with the same relentless battle to provide for their families. Nevertheless, getting enough money to put food on the table was a struggle at times. I do know that, on some occasions, food was so short in our house we only had bread and milk, sweetened with sugar to fill us up. In those early days, bread, milk, and some kind of sweetening, along with cheap cuts of meat and vegetables, was kind of a staple diet for us. Mother learnt to bake a very reasonable bread and butter pudding that really tasted good and was something to look forward to, unlike her treatment of vegetables, which were mainly boiled and boiled. Mildred has told me that occasionally she was sent to the butchers to get bones for the dog; these bones were then stewed up with whatever vegetables could be scrounged up and served with bread for the main meal.

Mildred also told me that early in the piece, Dad used to pawn his suit occasionally to tie the family over until the next source of income came along. Pawnshops were very prominent in those days.

Over time, conditions gradually improved for the family due to more regular employment and income, enabling us later on to enjoy more than just the bare necessities of life and the occasional toys and fruit at Christmas.

Sometime during the mid-thirties Henry, and then later Mildred, got employment, which would have eased the financial strain enormously. One thing about our father, despite the early setbacks, he tried hard to provide for his family; he was a genuine family man. The less than satisfactory diet of our younger years didn't seem to harm us in the long run; we all ended up tall, and we all dodged the worst of the childhood diseases prevalent at that time.

At the end of Davington Road, they were still building houses when we arrived, and a new school was built there further round the bend. That was the first school I went to; how long I attended that school I don't recall, but I do know that we moved to Cannington Road before World War Two started in 1939. I then went to school in Dawson Road.

I could read very well for my age and was learning to write. Being left-handed, I remember it was at that school in Davington Road where I was told I must use my right hand for writing. It must have been policy to convert left-handers over to the right hand because teachers were consistent at it. I remember the schoolteacher standing over me saying, 'We must use the other hand for writing,' and quick to reprimand when I relapsed. Eager to learn at that age, I complied with what I was told. These days, I find I am somewhat ambidextrous: still right-handed for writing and most things designed for right-handers, but left-handed for throwing things. Another thing I remember was that classes were mixed, whereas the remainder of my schooling was in boys only schools.

THE TOT'S VIEW OF THE WORLD

Scrambling about in the hazy distant mist of my mind, some of my earliest vague memories occur around from the age of about four.

The street was a three or four-year-old's mirror of the world; events outside the family home happened there, and the receptive brand-new mind of a child took it all in. People walked; workers and tradesmen passed by; cats and dogs ran across, and vehicles drove down the road; everything was a fascinating new learning experience.

The child was not to know the world changing events taking place in the real world. The machinations of Hitler and Mussolini, and the rise of fascism; Franco and the Spanish Civil War; clashes between British fascists and communists; or the abdication of the British king. No, his horizon was limited by the row of houses at the end of the street; his home, the sanctuary. Family; porridge with golden syrup; bread and strawberry jam. There were too many interesting things outside to wonder at and learn. His knowledge of the wider world would come later. As mentioned earlier, there was a lot of building work still going on around the Davington Road area (and no doubt all over Dagenham) and it was always an irresistible magnet for growing children. How inquisitive and fascinated we children were with all the building work going on and the struggle the watchmen had to keep us away and clear from danger. As children, we couldn't see the danger, only the interesting, exciting activity going on.

A not so funny incident I remember concerned Edwin. We were watching a workman melting bitumen over a brazier and Edwin, ever curious, went to touch the almost liquid tar.

'Don't touch that!' the workman shouted as Edwin, screaming, withdrew his already scolded finger.

Night watchmen protected the building sites at night; they used to sit in a hut in front of the building site. They always had a coke-filled brazier in front of the hut and in the winter evenings we would stand around the brazier keeping our hands warm and talking to the watchman if he would let us, until our mothers called us home. How these watchmen (who were generally elderly men) survived the cold nights I don't know, but they did and no doubt the income was sorely needed.

One particular watchman, who was a favourite of ours, was Chinese. He used to regale us with entertaining stories of his past, forever declaring how much cleverer the Chinese were compared to us lot. He told us about the Chinese language, and that how the same word, spoken in different tones, could mean different things. Very superstitious, he warned us never to have our photograph taken; he believed that the camera had an evil eye and if someone took a picture of you, they take part of you away. He said raindrops were little devils, and that's why everyone runs away when it rains. The Chinese man was not always at the same site, but it was always a pleasure when he was at our local one; he was so entertaining.

Most of the sand and gravel for the huge building project was obtained locally. In our area it was excavated from two large pits excavated between the railway and Mayesbrook Park.

Some enterprising people, and forward-thinking councillors, had already thought up a use for these pits and that was for them to be turned into boating lakes for public use. Work had already commenced to provide access to the lakes, via Lodge Avenue, until the war put a stop to it and it was fenced off. Even though access to the lakes was forbidden, these lakes were to provide an important part in our activities during the war years, as you will read later.

In those days, the streets of every town had lots of activity during the day: doctors, tradesmen and itinerant vendors generally travelled down working-class streets. Traffic was light, and it was relatively safe for children to cross them and play in them; unlike today, where travelling through endless suburbs and down countless empty streets with silent houses, the people are not to be seen. Car is king.

In the 1930s, the era I am talking about, working-class people generally used public transport, rode a bike or motor bike, or walked. It was never envisaged that motor vehicles were for the workers; therefore, the streets were relatively narrow with no provision for garages at the houses, which were mostly terraced, though there was the occasional break between the rows – the lucky ones were those at the ends with a side entrance. The era of consumerism came later on, after the end of the Second World War, when the factories, geared up for the war effort and inundated by returning servicemen, had the means to keep up with the demand, resulting in cars becoming affordable to most workers. As mentioned before, the houses all had a back garden and a tiny front garden bordered by a privet hedge fronting the street. Because the streets were too narrow for cars to park on both sides, unfortunately, the front garden and the privet hedge had to go to accommodate the family car. Then the folly of the narrow streets became obvious.

Back to the thirties; for a child of about four or five allowed out alone for a short time, perhaps my earliest memories are of exploring the street where we lived watching the passing parade, making friends with the new boy down the road, showing off by wrestling, or climbing the lamppost outside the house. There was no sense of fear at that age. Remembering the squabbles between my mother and the woman next door; over what, I don't recall. Once, during an argument, our mum was pushed into the rose bush; I remember her later indoors, muttering 'ouch' while pulling out the thorns sticking in her thighs. One day, I found some dog biscuits and tried to convince the boy next door, the son of the fighting mother, to eat them, unsuccessfully. I was hoping that if he did, he would turn into a dog. I had a vivid imagination, even then.

Even though the streets were relatively quiet, I had my first accident in life on Davington Road, I was run over by a motorcycle down the bottom of the street; apparently, I was trying to race it across the road. My scalp was opened badly by the accident, and I have always carried the scar from it; it was noticeable after a short haircut.

To a preschool child's eyes, there was a never-ending procession of the passing parade that traversed the street and, indeed, all the other streets of Dagenham. Daily, there was the milkman and the baker, from several rival firms, calling around with their small electric vans or electrically propelled cars. Weekly, there was the greengrocer and the hardware man selling, as well as other essentials, the all-important paraffin oil for the heaters. On Fridays, Dad would come across with a penny or so for a visit to the confectionary seller, who cleverly timed his drive down the road on the afternoon of payday. There were shops that sold these things of course, but the lot of the housewife in those far off days was to trudge daily to the shops to buy food for their family; the convenience of the street vendor was for some, hard to resist.

Another conveyance, for many of these vendors, was the horse and cart, and one can't have horses without manure, so it was the duty of the children with garden-proud dads to be ready at the front gate with bucket and spade in case the horse dropped something. When that happened, there was a scramble by the children to see who could get there first.

Others to call, included: the rent man with his brown satchel hurrying from door to door; the insurance man on his motorised bicycle, and the fishmonger, who usually called on a Sunday. Whoever can forget the vendor calling out 'Cockles! Mussels! Fresh Shrimps!' On summer weekends, the ice cream man called too.

Then there was the coalman. Every house had a coal cellar under the stairs, and the coalman would call on a regular basis. Wearing his thick canvas coverall, with a hood black with coal dust giving off an earthly smell, he would carry in a 1cwt bag of coal on his shoulder to dump in the coal cellar under the stairs. With the coal fires of course there had to be the chimney sweep; a surprising amount of house fires were caused because people didn't keep their chimney flue clean. When yours was due, he would come in, put a cloth over the fireplace and work the chimney brushes up and down the chimney. if you were unlucky, a particularly hard bit of soot would come down suddenly, and whoosh, a rush of air sent soot into the lounge room; this meant a bigger clean up than normal. Some people kept the soot to put on the garden in spring; it was supposed to be good for onions.

Another industrious caller in the thirties was the window cleaner; his task was popularised by a pre-war song sung by George Formby titled, 'When I'm Cleaning Windows.' There was plenty of regular work for the window cleaner in the grubby air of London.

Monthly or quarterly visitors were the gas meter reader, and the electric meter reader. The meters were inside the house. The gas meter took pennies, and the electric meter took shillings. Whenever there was a robbery from the meters, the housewives would gather around muttering and gossiping about 'Flannel Foot'. This was the local vernacular for a person, mythical or not, who was believed to go around at night, his feet muffled by flannel, creeping in and out of houses robbing the meters and anything else that could be taken from a house during the night. I never heard of Flannel Foot ever being caught. Later, I used to speculate about Flannel Foot and wonder whether he was sometimes a convenient scapegoat for some light-fingered tenant at the burgled residence.

Occasionally, the knife sharpener would come around on his tricycle; the one I remembered the best was an Irishman with the friendly smile, up to date with latest gossip and jokes, as he worked away on his pedal-powered grinder.

Home birth was common then and often one would see the busy midwife cycling silently on her errand, and the doctor buzzing about in his car.

Periodically, council workers would come down to clean the street and the drains.

Sometimes, to the delight of the children, would come the man with the horse and cart pulling a hand operated Merry–Go–Round, the man giving children a ride for a jam jar; a short ride for half pound jar, longer one for a pound jar. Then there was the 'rag and bone man' who, besides rags and bones, would collect any unwanted household items that perhaps he could sell on for a profit. Returning in my middle twenties, I was delighted to hear the Rag and Bone man still doing the rounds and still singing the same call, 'Ole rags, penny a pound for ole rags, O.' No doubt, you would get more than a penny a pound for your old rags later in 1956. Sometimes, a singer would walk down the street hat in hand begging for money. My mother said they were leftovers from the Depression and should go out and get a job.

So, every day of the week, people of diverse occupations visited the child's street, in addition to the local residents; the worker going to work; the housewife gossiping and shopping, and the children going to school. This activity was an important part of the growing child's education, portraying several aspects of society outside of one's family. Adding to this further, education included walks to the local shops at Becontree or the Robin Hood, and bus rides to the larger centres: in our case, to the town of Barking.

In the 1930s, people had fewer food choices, walked and cycled more, and were a lot leaner than later in the century.

I know that Father was quite pleased with himself for his family's move from London to Dagenham, even though it was a move of only about ten miles; it was a move from the grimy, overcrowded slums of London to a new suburb with new houses and a new start in life. I think he went to great lengths extolling the virtues of the place whenever relatives visited. I can understand his enthusiasm after learning of his history of the Great Depression and the disappointing migration to Canada, but for us the, young toddlers, though we had a cleaner, safer upbringing, Dagenham had a bit of a stigma attached to it.

Those of us with little to no education, or qualifications, found it difficult to find work from some employers other than labouring jobs. I came across potential employers who when told our place of abode, sneeringly remarked, 'Dagenham, aye, can't you find work at Fords?' I must admit, though, it didn't help our task when you consider we had the most appalling speech and grammar.

Among the working people, there was still a touch of class discrimination even amongst themselves. However, that was the future; for the present, we youngsters were settling in the new community and enjoying the clean air and space we had all around. The pressures of adulthood, teenage years, and prejudice were still a long way off.

I recall hot lazy pre-war summer days when aunts and uncles would visit us in Dagenham. Aunties would descend on us and cover us in wet kisses; no matter how hard we tried, we couldn't avoid the wet kisses. Uncles asked questions we couldn't find answers to and always we heard the same exclamation.

'Look 'ow big you are now! My! 'Aven't you grown.'

'Look 'ow big he is 'arry.'

Uncle would pass some remark such as 'Been fighting with the boy next door yet? Put up your mitts.'

Though other relative's visits weren't all that frequent, the more frequent visitors were Uncle Harry, Mum's brother, and Aunt Vi. They lived in Stratford, London; they had three boys, Harry, Joe, and Ron.

When the cousins came with their parents, and seeing their ages were similar to ours, the result was usually a lot of lively talk and squabbling. Any arguments that got too boisterous were quickly quietened with a stern reprimand from the adults.

Uncle Harry would always generously give us a shilling piece to spend as we liked, even though they were just as poor as we were; perhaps the reason was to get us out of the house for a while. I must add, though, that was when their children weren't with them.

Uncle Harry, Aunt Vi and their three children in the backyard of Davington Road.

***

Housing was funny in England; though it was noted for long wet and cold winters, they never seemed to build houses suitable for the climate. Every winter, as soon as a severe cold snap set in, one would hear stories of frozen pipes and burst water mains. In Davington Road, our house had only one decent built-in fireplace – which was for the front room – so on cold winter evenings, the whole family would crowd round the fire trying to keep warm while listening to the radio, reading or playing records. A two-bar electric heater was another source of heat, but that could only be put on when Dad was present; normally, it was only used in the kitchen at breakfast time.

Up in the bedrooms, the fireplaces were too small to be of much use, and dangerous for children to be left alone with. The heating was provided by paraffin oil heaters, which were notorious for sending off noxious fumes and dense smoke if the wick was not trimmed right. No doubt, the oil heaters took some of the chill out of the air, but the warmth emitted was suitable only for undressing and changing into nightwear, and probably just as dangerous as the open fireplaces. I remember being woken up one night and being ordered out of the bedroom. In the light, I could see my brothers' faces all covered in black soot and I burst out laughing at the sight, they in turn pointing to my face and laughed at my black face. The wick had been turned too high and a dense pall of black smoke poured out of the lamp while we slept.

During the cold nights of winter, when frost was about, the condensation from our breathing would freeze on the windowpanes, leaving a curious feathery pattern somewhat like ferns. 'Jack Frost' had been around doing his artistry they told us. It was also an indication of how freezing cold the bedrooms really were.

If snow was expected during the night, we would jump out of bed in the morning and, with our fingernails, scratch through the ice on the windowpane to look out. It was a wondrous thing if snow had fallen. The whole world seemed to have changed. Sounds were muffled, the air felt warmer, and everything was covered with a blanket of white clean snow. Gone were the dark and dreary surfaces of yesterday. In its place was the brilliance only a blanket of snow could provide, and the expectation of the fun and games we could play in the snow; if the snow didn't melt or become mushy by afternoon. Generally, the freezing conditions would re-establish itself soon after the snow, the ice creating dangerous conditions for pedestrians and vehicles alike.

Nobody we knew had fridges in those days and, at Christmas, the cold nights were put to good use for setting the jelly. Of course, care was taken to make sure cats couldn't get to it.

Christmas time is a time of magic for children as the stores fill their windows with extra goodies and coloured lights, and at home preparations made to cook the Christmas pudding and the mince tarts. The atmosphere of Christmas was infectious to us children as we go to bed on Christmas Eve in anticipation of what tomorrow will bring. The Christmas stockings were filled with apples and oranges, (oranges were something of a delicacy) and a couple of metal wind–up toys, made in Japan. These usually never lasted past Christmas Day but, as children, we never knew any better anyway, so we enjoyed them on the day and also enjoyed the extra food that was on the plate for that one day of the year. Included, perhaps, in the stocking were a few sweets and chocolates and a game of some sort, and that was the extent of the Christmas presents.

The wonderful food was a welcome change too. For the only time of the year, we had such foods as roast chicken or turkey, followed by the obligatory plum pudding into which was put three-penny bits for one to find, followed again by mince pies and Christmas cake; a banquet for that one day of the year.

The three-penny bits were something to be careful of when eating the plum pudding; I'm sure that a few people swallowed the things on that day. We managed to come through unscathed.

The family in the backyard of Davington Road.

Henry pushing the car with Dennis in it; myself with hands on hips; Pat front left.

Mildred holding Edwin. Second picture: Mum and Dad with Pat. Baby Edwin.

***

The larger shopping centre to Davington Road was at the 'Robin Hood,' so named after the public house there. Being new, and catering for the newly arrived families eager to furnish their new homes, the appliance and furniture stores sold the latest at the price range that working people could afford, on terms, naturally, and our family was no exception. It was a pleasant walk to the shops because the route took us past Mayesbrook Park and next to the toilets was a children's playground, further over was the bandstand and on some Sundays in summer a band would play there. In the opposite direction, with fewer shops but equal distance away, was another shopping area; the 'Round House,' also named after its local public house. It never had the same larger choice of appliance stores as the Robin Hood.

I think it was from the Robin Hood where most of our household appliances and kid's toys were purchased. Sometimes, a trip by bus to Barking was taken to compare prices and the latest trends.

The pride and joy in our house was the radiogram, a large cabinet in mahogany containing a record player and radio, and facing it was the sofa. I remember the radio was turned on most of the day, every day. Turning out the popular songs of the day, such as 'Who's Afraid of the Big Bad Wolf?', 'Stormy Weather,' and 'Cheek to Cheek,' as well as the usual sloppy, sentimental songs of that era. Also popular at the time was the singer Paul Robson, and the military band music of Phillip Sousa churning out the latest marching songs. Very appropriate considering the unrest and the increased military build-up of those days.

Mildred had her own wind up gramophone, so could play her choice of music.

An unhappy event concerning the sofa was to occur. When Mother went shopping, she usually dragged us younger kids along with her unless someone older was in the house; this particular day, the two youngest were left at home while I went to the shops with Mum. On returning home, we discovered the lounge room full of smoke and the back of the sofa smouldering; the kids had been playing with a piece of burning coal from the fire and dropped it behind the cushions. It was quickly put out, with a jug of water, but the sofa (Mum and Dad's pride and joy) was now marred by the hole burnt in the back. My mother, when relating that incident, for years after that (actually, all her life), for some unknown reason, always maintained that it was I that burnt the sofa. I can still hear her voice when gossiping to one of the neighbours, 'He's very naughty Frank is you know; he even burnt a hole in the back of our new sofa.'

Sometime in the mid-thirties, Henry got a casual job with the Hardware man who travelled around the streets in a lorry. It must have been a handy bit of income for Henry, and a relief for Father with one less to give pocket money to. I recall once when Henry bought a cheap old motorcycle and took me for a thrill ride on it, we were going over to the Thames flat, which in those days was just open fields with grazing cattle. I was surprised when, all of a sudden, he drove onto a grass reserve and laid it down on its side and shouted to me to get down and hide. I woke up to what was happening when I saw a police car drive by; Henry didn't have a licence.

In these days of the mid-thirties, my memories, apart from visiting the local shops and parks, are of bike trips into the country, of train rides to Barking and, rarely, into London to Regents Park Zoo or some other event. Though the financial situation had improved marginally for the family, it was still a strain on the budget to provide anything but the bare essentials; not that a five-year-old boy had any conception of these matters.

So, the Kelly family moved along, a growing family living their life the best they could on a council worker's wage; the children enjoyed themselves nevertheless (apart from sometimes catching one of the common childhood illnesses of the 1930s), unaware of the more pressing concerns of the adult mind. Again, a five-year-old wouldn't know anything about the world's political situation. He wouldn't know that just when the country was coming out of the worst financial disaster ever, and the people and the economy were recovering and looking forward to prosperous times ahead, another war was looming, threatening to undo it all. There were plenty signs of prosperity for some. New private housing estates going up on the outskirts of London; a trip to the new Southend Road showed large volumes of traffic, with the attendant traffic jams at some intersections.

BICYCLE FAMILY

We were a bicycle family. When we were of a certain age, we were presented with our first child's bicycle, and it was the duty of the next eldest son to push us around the streets until we learnt how to ride and balance on our own. At the age of about six, that probably only took two times round the block. From then on you were on your own and, as confidence grew, so one was able to venture a bit further afield, under parental restrictions of course; perhaps as far as the local shopping centre, avoiding the main road as much as possible. Riding in the parks was out because of the rules forbidding cycling. There were no laws regarding safety helmets, but strict rules about lights and reflectors when riding at night, though we children were not allowed out after dark anyway.

We were a different family compared to most on the estate. Whereas others would play in the parks or in the streets, on fine weekends, we would get away from the housing estate and enjoy a ride in the country; in those days, there was still plenty of country around. Earlier on, on summer weekends when the weather was fine, the family would take off for a picnic ride. Mum and Dad on the tandem bike, with two children in the attached sidecar; Henry, with one in a chair on the back of his bike (I think it depended on weight which child went where) and Mildred and Pat on their own bikes. Some of these trips went as far as Epping Forest. These longer rides involved several stops on the way; sometimes alongside an apple orchard where Dad would smooth talk the farmer into giving us some apples.

When I got old enough and could handle my own bicycle competently, I lost my comfortable ride and travelled the road in convoy with the others, relieving the parents from some of the weight. I remember pedalling like mad trying to keep up with them as we departed for a trip to Hainault Forest or Ockendon Wood; later, it was Dennis's turn and so on. In a large family such as ours, consisting mainly of boys, there was naturally a strong sense of machismo which made one want to prove himself just as strong and capable as the other, so we were quick and eager to take our place in the family bicycle hierarchy. Along with our riding lessons, came also the responsibility of looking after the bike, such as cleaning and pumping up the tyres.

Though the bike rides were sometimes long and tiring for our young bodies I believe, in the long run, they went a long way in strengthening not only our bodies, but also our hearts and lungs and stood us in good stead later in adult life. Mother was fond of saying,

'My boys grew tall and healthy because they always ate their porridge every morning.'

However, I think the credit should also go to the strenuous exercise we were getting when cycling.

The acquisition of a bicycle also gave us more freedom to explore the surrounding area later on, when our bodies were stronger, remembering, of course, there were fewer cars on the roads.

There are several family photographs of that era showing us having fun in Epping Forrest and the different configurations of sidecar attached to the tandem.

Frolicking in Epping Forest

The bikes were also handy for any of those little errands to the shops. I recall one incident; it might seem funny now but, at the time, no one thought it so. There was no sugar for breakfast and Mildred declared that she wasn't going to work unless she had sugar for her porridge and her tea, and she was already late. Therefore, I was sent to the Round House shops. It was that time of the year when the gale-force westerly winds blew; on the way back, with a thirty-knot westerly pushing me along and a pound of sugar tucked in my jumper, I couldn't slow down for the left-hand turn. I had to take from Porters Avenue and, sure enough, I came off the bike – the bag of sugar landing in the middle of the road and bursting open. I scraped up as much of the sugar as I could into the busted bag, which by then only amounted to about a quarter of the pound, and carried on homeward. Unfortunately, on the remainder of the journey, a lot of the sugar spilled out through the tears in the bag and, by the time I got home, only a few rather dirty spoonfuls of sugar were left. You can imagine the uproar from everyone faced with a sugarless breakfast because of my carelessness.

HULLBRIDGE

During the latter part of the 1930s, the family used to take a week's summer holiday at a town called Hullbridge, on the river Crouch. The memories of the smell of salty air, wonderful days spent in the thundery summer sun would last for a long time. We would rent a cottage and spend a few happy days fishing or crabbing. In front of the grounds surrounding the cottage, a bell tent was erected for meals and for the children to sleep in if it was fine weather. I remember the family hiring a boat one day and being caught in a thunderstorm; in our scramble to get back to shore before the worst of it hit, some of us fell in at the river's edge, so ended up getting wetter than if we had been caught by the rain. Another time, Henry caught a few crabs and put them in the tent for the night, but during the night some found their way into the cottage and we were awakened by Mother's screams as one crawled onto her bed. She was always terrified of anything natural that walked, ran or crawled.

Our holiday cottage at Hullbridge

Bell Tent beside holiday cottage

In a way, our Hullbridge holidays were more memorable to me, perhaps, in that being older, I could appreciate them better. They were also the last major times we as a family had fun and bonded before the deprivations and forced separations of the impending war.

WAR TALK

There was lots of talk about war in those days too. As well as the threat from Germany, the Spanish Civil War was still raging and the Japanese were going amuck in China. In contrast, King Edward VIII abdicated and King George VI was crowned.

I remember a crowd of youths marching down the street arm-in-arm chanting, 'We want war. We want war,' and Mother darkly saying, 'They'll be sorry if we ever do have war, they don't know what it's all about.' Woolwich Arsenal was not too far away across the river Thames and they seemed to be forever testing ammunition; the booms echoed through the air. In addition, of course, being England, there were plenty of long boring days when it seemed to rain incessantly. I noticed that when the rain was constant, the raindrops increased momentarily every time an explosion occurred, heightening the dullness of it.

In 1938 or early 39, just about as we were moving from Davington Road, I recall seeing workmen digging out foundations and building air raid shelters on strategic corners.

Our father was a political person, and a sceptical one, who never took things at their face value and would debate their merits one way or another and oftentimes he would sit at the dinner table pontificating on the current political scene to adult members of the family or any other adult visitor who happened to be present. That's one reason, perhaps, why we all grew up sceptics ourselves. The frantic excavations for air raid shelters would have prompted him to say, 'I wonder who's making money out of this?' I remember once as we were walking in a family group to look at the Cannington Road shelter, a practice air raid warning sounded, and Henry started to run and said jokingly, 'Quick, get in the shelter.' We all laughed thinking it a huge joke, not realising that before too long it would be deadly serious. Around this time, there was also an increase in the country's display of military readiness. Mildred took us to one demonstration at Hornchurch Aerodrome, and apart from much flying around by planes, I remember seeing a hut blown up by a well-placed bomb at the edge of the runway.

MOVE TO CANNINGTON ROAD

The house at Davington Road was really too small for a growing family. With such a large family, the sleeping arrangements left a lot to be desired. I'm not sure where Mildred slept, but we three youngest ones slept in the same bed.

We were given the larger house in Cannington Road to rent where, incidentally, my parents lived for the next thirty odd years. At last, Mildred had her own room and the five boys in the second bedroom. Then the sleeping arrangements were less complicated. Henry, now in his late teens, probably had one of the younger kids in his bed. Pat entered our bed from the other end with his feet somewhere about our waists. Later, when both Henry and Mildred were away in the army, Pat slept in Mildred's bedroom. When either of them was home, Pat had to come back to our room. If both Henry and Mildred were home at the same time, it was back to the old sleeping arrangements.

Father would proudly boast we had the best house in the street because it was semi-detached and built on the bend in the road – we could see right down the street to Porters

Avenue, whereas the other houses could only look at those opposite. Our dad, a keen gardener as he was, set to straight away planning his garden, putting in a birdbath and erecting the trellis for the roses. He discovered a large cache of sand buried in the back garden that came in useful for building the fishpond, and for any other future project that required sand.

When Uncle Harry and Aunt Vi visited, we would all sit outside in the back garden and drink tea and eat a piece of cake; Uncle Harry would give us kids a shilling piece and tell us to go for a walk and spend it on sweets or something. One day, my younger brother Dennis and I decided to take a ride on a train, so we walked to Becontree Station and bought a ticket to the next stop, which was Upney, then walked from there back home. It was really a long journey for young boys of about eight and nine and probably our first adventure. By the time we got back, it was getting late and all the family was starting to get frantic. We all know the result; Mother giving us a telling off while Aunt and Uncle were saying,

'Leave them alone, they didn't know they were going to be late.' Mostly, everyone was happy that we had come home safely.

After moving to Cannington Road, Dennis and I had to change schools to the Dawson Road School. The major memories of that change include being introduced, for the first time, to gas masks. Children were each issued with one and we had to practice putting them on and leaving them on for extended periods. This was very traumatic for most of us because breathing was very difficult; the smell of the rubber was unpleasant, and the eyepiece quickly became clouded with vapour making the whole experience frightening. Even at that young age, I was certain that I couldn't keep them on long enough to be of any use because I found it impossible to breath in them. Nevertheless, all people were issued with them and we carried them around every day for the next year or two.

We had lectures about anti-personnel mines. They apparently thought the Germans were going to drop and we were told not to touch any metallic object that looked like a toy or a butterfly type of thing. We had these lectures regularly throughout the war.

The government then issued to every household within the expected bombing range, a prefabricated air raid shelter that was to be put in the back garden. They were called Anderson Shelters. These were made out of heavy-duty, corrugated iron and were large enough for a medium size family. The idea was to dig a hole, half the depth, erect the shelter in the hole, and place the earth dug out on top of the shelter. Another type was issued to households that either didn't have a garden or were further away from the expected bombing range. Neither would be of any use with a direct hit, but good protection otherwise. In our case, it was used as a handy garden shed, but more on that later.

As kids, I think we knew something bad was happening; we were not sure what it was, but were soon to find out that life as we knew it was about to be changed.

WOOLAVINGTON

The surprise came one day when we were all told at school: we were being evacuated to the country, away from London. To me, it seemed dramatic and unexpected because I don't remember ever being pre-warned. We arrived on the appointed day with our packed suitcases.

The passage of events is hazy in my mind, but I do recall all of the children were assembled at the school in class groups along with our suitcases and gas masks; all the mothers were hovering around saying their goodbyes, and then driven to the railway station. I think Dennis and I were in a state of confusion. We joined the steam train at Paddington Station; the station absolutely thronged with children and their minders. We learnt that we were going to Somerset and though we were told the name of the place we were going to several times, we couldn't remember it on the train. Pat was evacuated to Western-Super-Mare, Somerset. Edwin wasn't evacuated because it was deemed he was too young to be separated from his mother.

That evening, my group arrived at a little village called Woolavington and was assembled in the school hall.

The hall was filled with chatter as the local people milled around selecting certain children who were then taken away. Dennis and I were absolutely mystified about what was going on; slowly, and surely, the number of children diminished until only a handful remained. I wondered why we weren't snapped up with the early ones and came to the conclusion that perhaps we weren't as adorable looking as them and maybe amongst the scruffiest. In addition, some people only wanted a single child. Eventually, one of the women came up to us and, closely scrutinising us, declared, 'I'll take these two.' We then met Mrs Whaites who was to become our foster mother and disciplinarian for the next two and a half years.

We were taken to a farmhouse in the village, opposite the Post Office and General Store, and after being introduced to the members of the family, Mr Whaites; their son, Morris, aged about 17; their daughter, Pamela, aged 19, and grandmother, we were given food, a bath and then promptly put to bed.

Those first few days were strange to us; firstly, we enrolled in the village school along with all the other new arrivals, and then introduced to the different ways of farm life and all the interesting things that make up a working farm. The teacher we had in the beginning was one of the women who chaperoned us in our journey from London; she would sometimes take us for walks in the countryside surrounding Woolavington and show us the variety of trees and herbs, and the animals and birds that lived in the hedgerows and alongside the road.

*The evacuees on one of their country strolls about Woolavington.
I am in one of the groups of three standing up, with the dark coat
and hair. Dennis hiding his face.*
Note the Gas Masks.

In the afternoons following school, the usual routine was Dennis and I went either with Morris to milk the cows in the pasture, or attend to other farm duties (though I admit we boys didn't do much more than collect the eggs, if the chickens had laid any). Because farming was an essential industry, Morris was exempt from armed forces duty, but he was in the Home Guard.

It may seem strange now but, in the summertime in those days, the cows were milked in the field where they grazed. Morris would turn up in the small lorry with a milk churn, galvanised buckets, a stool and a leg rope; the cows were quite used to this and after the dog had rounded them up, they would (usually), patiently stand still to be milked. Morris was a happy fellow and, when milking, would sing the latest hit songs at the top of his voice, songs such as 'Run Rabbit Run,' 'Bless them all,' 'Mr Franklin D Roosevelt Joe,' and the cows would all stand around listening, quietly chewing their cud.

Living on the farm was a huge leap from the pavements and concrete roads of Dagenham: the smells of the country, the freshly mown hay and sweaty horses, and the cackling of the hens as they scratched in the straw, searching for the eggs of the broody one and milk fresh from the cow. All signs evocative of farm living. We had great fun running about the field and chasing the dog. Even though we were used to riding out into the countryside beyond Dagenham, most of the time the horizon was limited by the rows of houses across the road or down the street. Our part of Somerset was very flat. Now our horizon was to the hedgerows or, in the distance, the funny little hill named 'Brent Knoll.' To us it was a whole new way of life from the one we had been used to and in the fresh air, out in the pastures, we felt a freedom never experienced before.

However, this freedom wasn't as complete as we had imagined for, within a couple of days, we soon discovered Mrs Whaites was quite a disciplinarian. We came back wet one evening due to running in the wet grass after a rain shower, she said we had to get the stick for being naughty and promptly picked up a thin cane and beat us a few times about the legs. We were to discover that the stick was her favourite method of punishment for any misdemeanours and if by some chance the stick broke, she would make us go and get another. In hindsight, we may assume she wasn't used to having two children as boisterous as we were compared to her own, now grown up, children.

They were practicing Christians and we had a strict regime to follow on Sundays. In the mornings, we had to attend Sunday school at the Norman church in the village, and there was no way you could get out of it because we were given a booklet, and after every session given a religious stamp to stick in it. Mrs Whaites scrutinised the stamp without fail and, sometimes, questioned us about the sermon we had received. She didn't discover some of the mischievous pranks we got up to after the service though, such as playing hide and seek among the gravestones or pinching biscuits from the Presbyterian Chapel that abutted the graveyard. In the evenings, all the family went to evening service.

On the outskirts of Woolavington was a family that didn't go to any church; we were instructed not to speak to them. In contrast to his wife, the farmer was the most mild-mannered person one could meet. In all the time we lived on that farm, I don't recall him ever getting angry or raising his voice. However, by the same token, he had (as it seemed to me) a cruel streak when dealing with domestic animals used for food. Regularly, we had chicken for dinner and his method for killing them or the ducks was always the same. He used a very thin and sharp pocketknife, and he would hang them up by the legs, and insert the knife inside the bird's beak to sever the artery inside the neck. They would then squawk and flutter until dead from loss of blood. Perhaps we city boys were too sensitive but that's the way they did things there. If a large animal was going to be slaughtered for the homestead, such as a pig, numerous government regulations were involved. Either a fair portion of it had to go the government, or the family meat ration was adjusted, but it just shows the difference between living in town or on a farm; the farmers were never short of meat, milk or eggs.

Once I went with Mr Whaites to Bridgewater, a large town nearby. Apart from picking up some supplies, he was getting a pig slaughtered and he wanted me to watch the process. It was pretty gruesome because the animal wasn't stunned before being hoisted up by the hind legs and having its throat cut. The terrified animal squealed a lot as it died from loss of blood. I said to Mr Whaites, 'I've never seen so much blood.'

He merely replied, 'You'd lose as much blood if your throat was cut.'

Across from the barn was a dark and deep, murky pond secured behind a low stone wall. I used to shudder every time I went past it. Into it would go all the kittens the cat had, or the remains of any other small animal that had died; I always associated the lake as a disturbing place of death, and can still recall the panic squealing of the kittens as they entered the water tied up in a Hessian bag.

As if to make up for the dark forbidding pond, the farm homestead area was a bird paradise. The various yards around the farm were surrounded by stone walls with lots of deep holes in which birds, such as Tom Tits, built their nests and reared their young; under the eaves of the house, Swallows and Swifts darted about catching food for theirs.

Beside the farmhouse was a walled garden where they grew vegetables for the kitchen. Mr Whaites used to smoke a pipe and often, when he was working in the garden, he would leave his pipe and tobacco in the tool shed. Sometimes Dennis and I would sneak in, stuff the pipe with tobacco and smoke it until we went dizzy. No wonder we took up smoking at an early age. The farm employed a farm labourer, Harry; a pleasant man of about fifty years of age, who lived on his own in a small cottage. He also worked in the garden sometimes besides doing his farm duties.

The Woolavington farmhouse (photo taken in 1990)

The first few months of the year went by fairly quickly because Germany hadn't started bombing England, so we soon settled down to life in the village and got to know all the other children at school.

Morris used to love shooting and early Sunday mornings, he would often take me with him to look for rabbits, hares, or ducks for the table, or any other game birds. When eating something shot with the shotgun, one had to be careful not to swallow one of the pellets that may have been left in the meat.

Morris was quite a competent shot and sporting with it. Once, he came across a fox cornered in a tree hollow; the terrified fox looked at us with a frightened look in his eyes.

I shouted, 'Shoot him, Morris!'

'No' he said, 'I'll give him a fair chance to escape'.

Morris fired but missed! The fox made off.

With the clear cleaner air, it seemed colder there during winter than it did in London and with more snow in winter. At night-time, the stars and the moon shone with extra brightness. At Sunday school, we were given more of the religious side to Christmas than we would have back home in London. I don't know that it made us religious though, probably less. I think our paths were already determined.

During winter when the geese came over from the artic on their way south, they sometimes landed in the grassy pastures to feed. When they were heard squawking overhead a cry would call out, 'Geese, Geese overhead' and some of the farmers, Morris most definitely, would rush home, grab their shotguns and either try to hit them in flight or find out where they had landed. Those lucky enough to get a goose went home well satisfied. Morris got one or two, and they tasted wonderful.

During harvest time, because of the shortage of labour, children who lived on farms were allowed time off school to assist. Dennis and I were a bit too young to be of much assistance, but we went anyway. I recall once being given the reins of a draught horse, ploughing a field, but the horse wouldn't obey my instructions and, I'm sure, deliberately tried to step on my foot. No way could I get him to walk down the furrow in a straight line so, after a few valiant attempts, the reins were taken off me.

It was exciting when the wheat was being cut. The harvester went around the edge of the wheat field, gradually reducing the amount of wheat to be cut; eventually, there was only about two rows left, and farmers stood by with their shotguns. We evacuee children were told to stand back not aware of what was about to happen, but soon found out. When the final rows were cut, the population of rabbits that had lived in the corn for months while it was growing started to panic. After the second last row was mowed, the rabbits tried to escape one-by-one, only to be shot by the hunters. As the last row was disappearing, rabbits by the dozen came pouring out, including dozens of their young. For the last bit remaining, the farmers put aside their shotguns and told us children to try and catch the babies, which we did, but plenty of them escaped to live another day.

Another exciting time for us was when the threshing was done. It was a large, noisy machine hired on contract and it seemed all the local farmers gathered around to give each other a hand on their respective farms. To my mind, it was an amazing machine. The sheafs of wheat were tossed in on the top, and quickly chaff poured out into bags at one end, and grains of wheat at the other; I just couldn't imagine how it worked.

Somerset is famous for its cider, and no self-respecting farm in Somerset would be without its cider apple orchard. The Whaites farm was no exception; there was a small apple orchard on the farm, from which they made their own cider. The apple press, and other paraphernalia, was in the cellar under the farmhouse. One day, home from school for midday lunch, Dennis and I found the outside cellar door was unlocked so we sampled a couple of glasses of cider; it was a couple of tipsy schoolboys who went back to school that afternoon. We both had trouble walking straight and trying to keep awake at school. Funny, that was the only time we found the cellar door unlocked.

By that time, the war had started in earnest and London was getting bombed relentlessly. The planes were bombing other targets including Bristol, which was only about 30 miles from us. Sometimes, at night, we could hear them going overhead. To lie in bed hearing the enemy bombers overhead, gave one an uneasy feeling. Morris was good at telling the type of bomber it was by its distinct engine note, some droned; 'That's a Junkers' he'd say, while others throbbed; 'that's a Heinkel or a Dornier,' he'd say. Looking towards Bristol at night, the red glow in the sky from the buildings on fire indicated where the bombs landed. It was an awesome sight.

One day a training plane, a Lysander, came down and crashed in a ditch near one of our fields. Morris rushed to it in the farm car and started syphoning out the fuel. 'Aviation fuel' he shouted, 'best fuel you can get.' While he was midway through the syphoning, a Royal Air Force Officer arrived and stopped him, making him return the fuel he had already put in the drum. Morris was very upset over that, but the officer couldn't be talked out of it.

Once or twice, our parents came for a day visit and, one day, Mildred turned up on leave from the army; I don't remember Henry visiting, he was probably stationed too far away. We would go for walks about the farm and village and catch up on all the news from home; about the bombing, and what Edwin was doing. Later, Dad and Mrs Whaites would get into earnest conversation, talking about what I don't know. Once, after our father, left Mrs Whaites said, 'Your father told a lie. He said London was bombed yesterday and it wasn't; otherwise, it would say so on the news.' She never lost a chance to find fault with us.

Dad was now a police officer in London, and Mum was working at the Ford factory in Dagenham. Factories now were on a war footing and engaged in either military vehicle manufacture or making munitions.

Even though we made new friends at school, and played and had fun, for the adults it was a different story and the atmosphere was rather sober. The war wasn't going too well on our side; Dunkirk had happened, Britain was losing battles everywhere, and being bombed relentlessly. The German planes seemed to be able to pick their targets at will despite the valiant efforts of the RAF. Whenever a convoy of troops passed through the village, the women were there handing out gifts such as chocolates, cigarettes and the like.

The war came to Woolavington one afternoon when a German plane, flying overhead, dropped its bombs harmlessly in a field just outside the village. We were standing in the drawing room when they came screaming down; Mrs Whaites in a panic, ordered us to climb under the kitchen table, the bombs landed while we were still scrambling to get under the table. The story went that the plane had mechanical problems on its way to Bristol and dropped its load prematurely to lighten its load. Everyone in the village must have gone to have a look at the craters.

A far more serious event occurred one afternoon when we were with Morris, while he was milking the cows in an outer field (though a portion of the outcome could almost be termed a comical farce, due to the actions of me and Dennis). Dennis and I were running around, as usual, and Morris was singing at the top of his voice as he sat on the stool milking; the cows stood chewing the cud thoughtfully waiting their turn.

A shadow or something overhead made me look up and there, as large as anything, was an aeroplane passing silently overhead with men tumbling out of it and parachuting down. I shouted to Morris, 'Look at that big plane!' He looked up astonished.

'That's a German plane,' he said.

The plane was very low and we could see the black German cross clearly on the side of the plane, and the men parachuting down. The plane vanished over the hedgerows and then we heard a crash as it hit the ground.

Morris rushed around gathering his stool and pouring his pails of milk into the milk churn and put them in the back of the lorry. He said the Home Guard, and perhaps the army, would be here shortly at the assembly point to round up the airmen and he will have to go with them, the rest of the cows will have to be milked later he said.

A little later, an army vehicle pulled up in the lane running beside our field, and the sergeant and a couple of others in uniform climbed out. Shortly down the lane, other men in civilian clothes riding bicycles came to join them. The sergeant quickly sorted out the squad and issued rifles to some. Before they went off, one of the men said to the sergeant,

'What about our bikes? If the Germans get them, they can ride off.'

He turned to us and said, 'If you boys see any Germans, pull the valves out of the tyres, and throw them away in the grass.'

I didn't know what a German looked like; all I knew was what the news propaganda people told us, that they were terrifying monsters whose main aim in life was to kill innocent English people.

'What do Germans look like?' I asked.

'If you see anyone dressed in a kind of light uniform' he said, 'they will be the Germans.'

Then off they vanished down the lane.

Silence for a while, and then in the distance we heard a couple of shots. A little while later, Dennis asked,

'Who are those people down the lane?'

At the far end of the lane, we could see a couple of people dressed in white slowly walking towards us.

Unsure whether they were wearing uniforms or not, at least their clothing was white.

'They might be Germans, take the valves out.' I said.

We both quickly did that and threw them into the grass, we watched as the couple came closer.

Then it became evident that they were an elderly couple dressed in whites taking an evening stroll.

About the same time, the lorry arrived with the prisoners and dropped off Morris and the men who had come by bike.

They went to their bikes; 'Hey my tires are flat,' said one, 'So are mine,' chorused the others.

'Where are the valves?' they asked, looking at us.

'We took them out because we thought they were Germans,' I said pointing at the elderly couple, 'we threw the valves in the grass as you said,' I added.

We left them searching frantically in the grass for their valves while Morris took us away to finish the milking.

The aeroplane crash was the biggest event ever to have happened in the area up to that period, so everybody from miles around went to have a look at the damage. The plane had just missed crashing into a farmhouse and ended up in its barn, destroying it completely. The story went that the pilot had aimed his crippled plane at a nearby ammunition factory before jumping out. The story could have been true because the factory was only about a quarter of a mile further on.

Every month, I had to write home to our parents to keep in touch and to inform them we were ok, and to advise them about what items of clothing we needed. Mrs Whaites supplied the envelope and stamp because we never had the money for such things.

By this time, we had been here two Christmases and were getting more homesick, especially since the discipline from Mrs Whaites was becoming more severe. I remember once I refused to eat my porridge because it was full of lumps and had been burnt. It made me gag when I tried to eat it. She said if I didn't eat it, I would have it for lunch; if I didn't eat it then, I would have it for dinner. Come dinnertime, I threw it in the fireplace when she wasn't looking. If the stick broke when Dennis or I was being punished, for whatever reason, she would send me to the bushes to get another. Naturally, I picked one as flimsy as I could.

Some of the local schoolmates knew of our beatings and I said to one I wanted to write home to my father about it without her knowing. I think his surname was Cox; there were many people in the district named Cox. He managed to get me an envelope and a stamp, and I wrote home telling our father how she was always hitting us and we wanted to go home.

Within a week father arrived at the farmhouse and said for us to get our things because he was taking us home. Naturally, we were overjoyed. I will always carry the memory of the taxi at the front of the farm, loading our suitcases in, and Mrs Whaites looking on silently while Mr Whaites, who always had a soft spot for me, gave me an embarrassing big hug and a sad goodbye. Morris had said goodbye in the house and said he would miss us, and that was the last I ever saw of them.

Many years later, about sixty in fact, I was to return to Woolavington and have a look at the old farmhouse and the village. It had changed, and what used to be the walled garden was now a housing estate. I was standing outside what used to be the post office taking a photograph of the house, when a middle-aged woman walked up. I asked her if this used to be the Whaites' house. She said it was, and I asked her if she knew Morris Whaites. 'Oh' she said, 'He died years ago from cancer.'

I thought it was very sad and decided not to stay any longer in the village.

BACK HOME

So, we were back home in Dagenham, and how our perceptions had changed after two years away. The rooms had been freshly wallpapered and painted; they seemed smaller than we imagined they were. The front parlour had folding doors separating it from the lounge room. It was the trend in that day and age for the parlour to be kept aside for visitors or special occasions, so for years there would be a quite useful room kept empty while we were squashed together in a pokey lounge room.

'Keep out of the parlour,' Dad said.

'Real posh,' I commented.

'Make sure it stays that way,' Dad replied.

The air surrounding Dagenham, indeed most of East London, was always hazy; polluted by smoke, exhaust fumes and a myriad of other pollutants. Growing up from a baby to an adult in that atmosphere, a person wouldn't notice it except if one had travelled and experienced better climates. The thickness of the air I had breathed in all through childhood come apparent to me, when midway through the war I returned from evacuation in Somerset. On our first day back, my brother, Edwin, who had stayed home through the worst of the 1942 bombings due to his young age, was eager to show Dennis and me the bomb damage in the surrounding area.

In Rugby Road, where the railway was bombed and the railway lines left hanging on the adjacent rooftops, there were shrapnel holes in the iron bridge. The flat down Cannington Road, where lived the old man who used to be always complaining about the noise we kids were making, was bombed-out. Our mother, probably about the first time she stuck up for us, would tell him he should be living on an island if he didn't like the sound of children playing. Edwin showed us other nearby bombed sites and their history.

It was evening and the late autumn sun was setting over the rooftops of the houses, the air was chill and their fires were burning; each chimney pot belching out a stream of smoke. The sun glowed with a deep red through the misty sky like a dying ember and the red reflection on the slate roofs, gave the scene an eerily artistic setting. The ruddy red of the sky, and of the roofs stretching to the near invisible horizon, was as if the fires of the blitz were still burning. Impressed, I said to Edwin, 'Why is the sky so red?'

He said, matter-of-factly, 'It's always red at sunset.'

'Hmm' I replied, 'I've never seen it so red.' We left it at that, but I was still intrigued by the amazing, fiery picture before me.

THE WAR CONTINUES

Back at the Dawson Road School, Dagenham, it was a challenge compared with the smaller, friendlier Woolavington School. Straight away, I detected a more machismo, intolerant type of atmosphere. It wasn't long before the more belligerent kids decided that any other who spoke with a hint of West-country accent was an object of fun. Now the age of about 11, I was tall for my age and fairly robust. The kids who tried me on landed flat on their backs, much to their surprise; my long reach played a good part of it, I must admit. I was not one who would shrink away from standing up for myself, even though I never went out of my way to confront anyone. The unfortunate consequence was that, though I was often being forced to defend myself and usually won, I got into trouble from the teachers for being 'a bully' even though it wasn't me that started the fight. Teachers in those days didn't bother to check the facts but were strong on discipline. Shortly after starting back at Dawson Road School, the time came for those of my age group to sit exams if they wanted to go to a higher-grade school rather than the low 'Elementary'. I was a bit nervous asking the headmaster about it seeing I was always in trouble with him, but Dad, who by now was an auxiliary police officer, brought the matter to a head by asking when I was going to sit the exam. So, I approached the headmaster, his name was Mr Comber; he looked at me sneeringly and said, 'You needn't bother, Kelly.'

Next term, I started at Bifrons Elementary School much to the disgust of Father, but he didn't bother to investigate further.

Dad in his police uniform

Life, generally, was pretty hectic for the adults at that period; the war still wasn't going too well on our side with fierce fighting in North Africa, and against the Japanese in Asia. While at sea, merchant shipping was taking a pounding from the German U-boats. However, owing to Germany's assault against Russia, the bombing over London had eased considerably; although, the Germans were still sending over the odd bombing raid at night, and the occasional rapid daylight raid. Our air-raid shelter was used as a garden-tool shed, as I mentioned earlier, and so during these night raids, we kids would sit up and watch whatever we could from our bedroom window until tiredness or the cold would send us to bed. Don't ask me what our parents were doing at the time because I don't ever recall them coming into our bedroom to see how we were. However, our father, an auxiliary police officer, was often on patrol during bombing raids and, apart from usual police duties, sometimes had to sound the air-raid siren, guard places that had been damaged, and go around at night checking that no lights were showing, and that people were inside.

The bedroom window faced west, towards London proper, so if the action was over the docks or the industrial area in the East End of London, which it generally was, we had a reasonable view from our small patch of sky.

I still remember full-moon nights, the rooftops shining in the moonlight, the air crackling cold, German bombers throbbing overhead and searchlights stabbing the night sky seeking them. The Ack-Ack guns blazed away from various positions, some nearby. A plane was caught in a searchlight, others immediately locked on, and then by triangulation, all flack was directed towards the target; it was an awesome sight.

Of course, what goes up must come down; therefore, soon after the blast from the shells, down came a rain of shrapnel; clanging, whistling and whirring around as it hit the road and the rooftops. Woe betides anyone caught out amongst it without adequate protection. For us children, it was strange feeling, a mixture of dread and excitement, a touch of shock if an explosion occurred nearby. On the one hand, we knew there was great danger but, at the same time, were fascinated by the drama of it.

Next morning at school, after a night air raid, the boys would gather around chattering about it and describing what they heard or saw. Not all air raids were witnessed, though; incredibly, some mornings we would go to school and the boys would say, 'Did you hear that raid last night?' However, we had slept through it and never heard a thing. One morning on the way to school, the streets, roofs and lamp-posts were festooned with long metallic strips; mystified, none of us could imagine what was the reason for it until one of the teachers told us it was dropped by German planes to confuse the radar. At that time too, another familiar sight in the sky were the Barrage Balloons sent up into the sky whenever an air raid was expected. Some were in stationary positions, others were attached by winch to the back of a truck, which could raise or lower them where required. Occasionally, one would break away in high winds and that would cause confusion and drama to the Air Force personnel in charge, who would go running around trying to track its progress and recapture it before the public did. These balloons were made from a durable waterproof material that was much sought after by people. Everything was in short supply those days, and this new material only available to the military – perhaps a forerunner of plastic.

One fearful night, I was awoken by a loud frightening whooshing sound; outside, was as bright as day and as by instinct, I found myself out of bed and halfway under it in my scramble for safety. My first thought was that the world had ended, but quickly comprehended it was a new weapon directed at the enemy. Looking out the window, I saw a large cluster of shells exploding around an enemy plane. The air raid defences were now using banks of rockets against the aircraft; any plane caught in their midst almost never stood a chance. One of these rocket bases was in Parsloe Park. Most of the other available ground in the park had been ploughed and sown with wheat; such was the shortage of food those days.

Reports from the radio and newspapers always exaggerated the number of German planes shot down compared to the Royal Air Force's losses, such as: 'Last night, the RAF shot down 59 German planes. The RAF only lost 5', so it was only guesswork on our behalf.

The Germans sometimes resorted to sudden daylight raids. I recall one morning, as I was getting ready for school, the air raid warning sounded and at the same time, the German bombers were screeching overhead and dropping bombs in the district. Houses in one cul-de-sac, Pear Tree Gardens, were destroyed for the second time in the war; we were completely taken by surprise and just stood there by the dining table, while the bombs were dropping. However, this was later in the war and, by this time, we children were becoming rather blasé about it unless we had boasting rights and could show we were there or had an interesting souvenir from it.

SOUVENIER HUNTING

Souvenir hunting was big in those days and every house had at least one souvenir to show off, some quite dangerous. We had a disabled incendiary bomb in our coal cupboard; at least, we assumed it was disabled. The irony of storing a very combustible weapon with highly combustible coal never occurred to anyone. I heard, years afterwards, that these incendiary bombs were quite capable of bursting into flames.

The danger of souvenir hunting was brought very much to our attention when I came in possession of some cannon shells. A German plane had crashed over on the Thames Flats, over towards Barking Power Station, and this time some of us children got there before the authorities. It must have been a constant worry for the authorities to get to crash sites or bombed areas before the souvenir hunters did. I noticed a belt of cannon shells amongst the wreck and grabbed a couple before anyone saw me. These shells were fired by the aircraft's gunner and were designed to explode on impact. They were about six inches long and one and a half wide.

Back home, I was pondering how I was going to set one off. I was aware how dangerous they were but was sure there was a firing pin mechanism that ignited them. I went into the air raid shelter/tool-shed and put one gently in the vice and very carefully unscrewed the head, exposing the firing pin. It seemed obvious to me then that all one had to do was strike the firing pin and the shell would go off.

I then took it outside and propped it upright against a low, decorative brick wall that separated the shed from the house and garden. Taking a concrete birdbath that was lying down on the ground, I leaned over and dropped it on the firing pin, making sure I was covered by the brick wall.

The explosion was dramatic as it echoed round the back gardens, and the dog next door went berserk; Mrs Alfreds opened the door to see what was going on, and the dog went charging in knocking pot and pans flying. She wasn't too happy, as you can imagine, but I promised untruthfully I never had another, though I wasn't sure of what I was going to do with the other one. The result: I was now, in the eyes of other children who possessed one, the expert on how to set off cannon shells. The remaining shell I decided to give to my friend, Jackie Short.

The next day, there was quite a hum going on amongst the couple or so boys at school who had one; wanting to know how to set them off. During the morning break, they set to jamming them in the toilet doors trying, unsuccessfully, to unscrew them. During the lunch break, one of the boys had managed to unscrew one, so a group of us ran over to a reserve not far from the school we called Matchstick Island – more about Matchstick Island, later. At the entrance, there was a double flight of stairs down to a ramp leading to the lake. The idea was to drop a piece of paving stone, from the top of the wall overlooking the flight of stairs, onto the firing pin; hopefully, setting off the shell. I was the expert, so I had the task of propping up the shell in the right place. With me was another boy, whose name was also Frank. The first attempt only knocked the shell over, so we ran down and propped it up again. We had only got halfway up the stairs when the boys started dropping pavers and, again, knocked it over. I was angry and called to them not to drop anything until we were back up behind the wall. We ran back, propped the shell up and turned to run up the stairs when the shell exploded. I felt the blast and pieces of shrapnel piercing my clothing, some cutting into my back, but I was wearing a heavy overcoat that protected me from the worst of it. I was very angry now and cursed the boys for again dropping things before we were safe, but they insisted they never dropped anything. It must have gone off by itself.

We started laughing about it as we started back to school, and they took turns in picking pieces of shrapnel out of my overcoat and going over the events of our escapade. Suddenly, one of the boys said, 'Where's Frank?' Realising he wasn't with us, we ran back to where we set off the shell and he wasn't there. On the ground and leading up one of the flights of stairs, there were spots of blood.

We went to his house, just past the school; his mother came out and said he was in bed, waiting for the ambulance. We went back to school in a state of unease, not sure what to expect. Back in the classrooms, I was idly watching out of the window towards the square of grass separating the rooms when I saw Jackie Short run into the centre and throw a smoking object onto the grass. Luckily, for him and others around him, his shell had not exploded, but had ignited and caught fire instead. He later told me he had been trying to unscrew the head by jamming it in his desktop, when it started smoking. During the uproar this episode caused, a police officer came around looking for me; when I was pointed out to him, I was taken outside and informed that because I had received cuts from the shell fragments, I too had to go hospital with the other Frank, to be assessed. I objected because I said I wasn't hurt badly but the police and medicos insisted. At the hospital, I was duly injected with anti-Tetanus and my minute wounds dabbed with iodine. I noticed that the other Frank was quite peppered with shell fragments on his legs and buttocks and was going to be kept in for the night; I was glad I was saved by wearing a heavy overcoat. I got back to school just in time to join them in the air raid shelter.

A bombing raid was going on at the time. The headmaster, Colonel Frank Jenks (Home Guard) as he liked to be called, was something of a disciplinarian and for the benefit of the rest of the schoolboys sheltering, gave me the usual lecture about explosives. I will relate later his idea of discipline and his methods of which these days would come under the heading of Dickensian and would probably lead to a criminal charge.

The raids by now were becoming less and less frequent as Germany became bogged down in Russia and had suffered reversals in North Africa.

Henry was now a radio officer in the Merchant Navy, as he had somehow wrangled his way out of the army; he was seldom at home and took part in various convoys across the Atlantic and, later, on the Artic convoys to Russia.

Mildred was now stationed in Scotland; sometimes, when she came home, it was with her boyfriend who I believe was an army butcher. She was very proud of the fact that her battery had shot down a German plane.

Life for a while became more settled and predictable and we read the papers and listened avidly to the radio for news about the war's progress.

Prior to 1939, most married women with children stayed at home to look after the children and to keep house, but now with the war effort in full swing all able-bodied adults were expected to take part. Most, like our mother, worked in factories turning out munitions, etc. The consequences of that, however, was that we four at home were expected to prepare the evening meal. These were days of strict rationing and the meat ration was such that a family of six got just enough meat coupons for us to purchase a leg of lamb once a week. Meat products that weren't on ration, if you could get them, consisted of sausages, liver or other offal. We generally managed to get hold of sausages; Dad insisted we got sausage meat because you got more of it. Therefore, most mid-week meals consisted of potatoes, cabbage and sausage meat. No wonder I often felt queasy after a meal. Pat, being the eldest and the more serious type, assumed charge and after much squabbling, Edwin, Dennis and I prepared the vegetables and Pat did the cooking.

For our efforts, we were given 1-shilling pocket money, which was used up in our weekly visit to the picture house on Saturdays to see the latest films, serials and cartoons. We used to go to the 'Electric' in Barking, colloquially called the 'Flea Pit'. One of the favourite weeklies among the boys was the Cowboy serial, 'The Range Robbers' staring, Bill Boyd as 'Hop-along Cassidy'. Another favourite was the 'Dead End Kids'; there were plenty of war films too that were pretty popular. Most of the kids from the Barking and Becontree area would have gone there.

The bus fare to and from was penny-halfpenny each way, and the entry fee into the cinema was nine pence. There were a couple of front rows in the Flea Pit for seven pence, but they were so close to the screen it was painful to look up at the film, so they were hardly taken.

TEIGNMOUTH

After the Blitz, many children from the first evacuation began trickling back to London. There came a time during the V1 episode when the authorities deemed it necessary to evacuate the children again. The exact date eludes me; I believe it was mid-1944, and the length of time escapes me also, but it was sometime before D-Day, 6th June 1944. We came back to London just before the V1 era ended. The common term for the V1 in London was 'the doodlebug'. Lucky for England, these weapons were not invented earlier because during the short time they were used, they caused a great number of casualties and a lot of damage.

Most of our Bifrons school group were sent to Teignmouth, a seaside resort in south Devon. I remember at Paddington Station, a porter asked me where we were going, I said Teignmouth; he sighed and said,

'Hah yellow sands, red cliffs and blue sea. Lucky you.'

I thought, 'how ridiculous, who ever heard of red cliffs?' However, when we got there, sure enough the cliff towering over the river mouth, locally called 'The Ness' was indeed red. Teignmouth was quite different from the hamlet of Woolavington, Somerset. Instead of farms with cows and chickens, we had fishermen cottages on the river and seaside hotels overlooking a sandy beach.

Teignmouth

We arrived at the town school where the usual selection process took place. There didn't appear to be any stipulation that siblings were to be kept together. A couple selected Dennis and Edwin and, before long, I was selected by Mrs Matthews, who was looking for a companion for her son, Reg, of the same age. I found out later that her husband was overseas in the Royal Navy.

It turned out I was lucky: the Matthews family were fishermen, they lived in a house on the waterfront of the river Teign; in fact, so close to the waterfront that on spring tides the water lapped the back steps. Even better, Reg had his own rowing boat moored outside the back door; the boat was fit for sailing, another learning curve for me – again, another exciting contrast for us Dagenham boys. Instead of hard pavements, or farms and cackling hens, we now had the salty seaside air, sand between our toes and squealing herring gulls. The town still had active, professional fishermen plying their trade on the river and sea. I watched them salmon fishing in the river, and on the beach near the river mouth where they rowed a net out to encircle the salmon, and then back on shore pull with all their might on the nets. Occasionally, a frightened fish would jump the net to freedom. There were no mechanical aids, and I marvelled at how they could row those large boats with equally large oars. I noticed among the weather-beaten older men, some had permanently curled hands; this was, no doubt, from all the hard-seafaring work. The huge whalebone arches placed along the esplanade evidenced the relevance of the sea to the locals.

The cottages backing onto the River Teign

So began a wonderful period, apart from school, of boating and fishing. A time where I learnt a lot about boating and fishing from Reg, who had spent his whole life around boats. Sometimes, he took on the role of a fierce sea captain and at other times, he was inclined to bully; despite this, we both got on well together. Natural seaman as he was, he regarded us city people as useless landlubbers.

Inside the river is a large sand shoal called 'Old Salty', only covered at high tide, over the centuries millions of cockles have been taken from there. The section of beach opposite where they are processed is composed entirely of cockle shells and, unless one's feet are especially hardy, it's impossible to walk over them without footwear. Anchored on the edge of Old Salty was a large raft with a mast and a bullseye on it; this was towed out to sea by the Royal Navy and used for target practice. One of Reg's tricks was to get someone to jump on the raft with the pretext of tying up the boat, then he would then pull away quickly leaving one stranded, sometimes for hours.

Inside the entrance, past the fishermen's boat sheds, was a slipway used to repair small naval vessels such as patrol boats or motor torpedo boats. Nearly every week, there would be one or two damaged boats, some flying the Cross of Lorraine, on the slipway. Only naval vessels and commercial boats were allowed in or out of the river mouth at night-time, and then they had to know the password, which changed every day.

The mouth of the river Teign had a very restricted entrance with a treacherous bar, and many a vessel large and small has met with disaster on it. When a storm was blowing, or the seas deemed too rough, the authorities flew a red flag on the promenade near the river mouth.

We did a lot of daytime fishing both inside and outside, if the weather was fine. The only bait we ever used were mussels taken from underneath Teignmouth Pier. In those days, there was no such thing as nylon or plastics, so the fishing lines were of fine twine with cat gut for the trace. If one didn't lay out your line neatly in the bottom of the boat, a huge tangle ensued. Sometimes, Dennis and Edwin came with us. I think Dennis will well remember the day we spent ages trying to get past the breakers, despite the red flag flying; eventually, we had to give up, much to the relief of the onlookers ashore. We were in competent hands; Reg was a master at reading the sea. Although the boat only had rowing capabilities, and Reg was only allowed to sail in the river, we still used to go out up to a mile. If far out, Reg was cunning enough to anchor near a motorised fishing boat, and as soon as we saw them starting up their motor or pulling up the anchor, we would quickly do likewise and call them for a tow back home.

Some mornings, Reg and I would go to the beach inside the river where the Herring Drifters unload their nets, and we would help in the expectation of getting some fish. They were only interested in herring, but sometimes they would accidentally catch the occasional whiting Reg would ask for these and, if given more than we could eat, Reg took them to the local fish and chip shop to sell the surplus; always the entrepreneur, even at that age.

The cliff face, called 'The Ness', on the western side of the river had a gun emplacement guarding the river entrance. In those days, only professional fishermen were allowed to use the entrance at night and there was a coded pass to get in, which changed every day. If a vessel tried to enter the river at night without the code, it could be blasted out of the water.

One fine afternoon, Reg and I were a long way out fishing near a motorboat and, as usual, when they began starting their motor we pulled over to cadge a tow. This particular boat had a faulty motor and no sooner did we start heading off when the motor conked out. This kept happening time and time again. At sunset, we still hadn't reached the bar; mindful of the necessity to know the code for a night entrance, the others in the motorboat called out to us if we knew the code. We said we didn't. By now, everyone was getting worried. Just on dark, finally, the motor fired into life and we made for the river entrance; the boat owner wildly flashed his torch up at the gun emplacement. A rifle shot ran out and we all scrambled for the bilges. Nothing else happened and we made the entrance and got home safely. We could only assume that someone up in the gun emplacement was having a laugh at us because all during our efforts to get home, they could see who we were.

I don't recall much about the school at Teignmouth, as it was, I was pretty much far behind with most lessons. I just tagged along. I do remember the teachers were much kinder and friendlier than at Bifrons, perhaps because they knew we were only there for a short while so they didn't worry about us.

For the first time during the war, I was truly happy. I was with a caring family, getting good food, and had a good companion with his own boat. It could not last and it wasn't going to last long but, before that, something important was about to happen that changed the whole course of the war.

Not long after we arrived, the town was becoming full of American servicemen. All the hotels fronting the promenade, locally called 'The Den', were occupied and on the promenade a large marquee was erected which was used as a cookhouse. The Americans were everywhere, offering us cigarettes or chewing gum if we knew where they could find any girls. One day, Mildred, on leave from the army, came on a visit with Mum and Dad; she looked quite smart in her ATS uniform. Everywhere we went, the Yanks would whistle at her; I think she enjoyed it very much.

At mealtimes, we used to hang around the cookhouse entrance hoping to get food the likes of which we hadn't seen since before the war. Reg did a newspaper-round on his bicycle. The Americans would buy a paper that cost a penny; they would hand over a two-shilling piece instead and, sometimes with a wave of the hand, not worry about the change.

One day after his paper round, Reg came flying home on his pushbike and said excitedly,

'The Yanks are gone!'

We went to the deserted promenade; the marquee had gone. Likewise, the hotels were empty! It was as though the whole town had been evacuated.

Wondering through the empty rooms, we picked up the occasional helmet, backpack or other discarded items not thinking of keeping them as mementos or souvenirs.

Unbeknownst to us, at that time, these men and thousands of others were now fighting for their lives on the beaches of Normandy, along with the Commonwealth and British forces. D Day had begun.

My happy idyllic existence was about to come to an abrupt end when Dad suddenly turned up and said he was taking us home. I didn't want to go but, apparently, Dennis and Edwin's foster parents were a fair bit older than Mrs Matthews and found having two boisterous pre-teen boys too much to handle. Dad said that seeing he was taking those two, I had to go too, back to the grim reality of wartime London.

I went back to Teignmouth, during the school holidays, in 1945 when Japan surrendered and was there for the celebrations. The main thing I can remember was that the promenade thronged with people; inhibitions relaxed, everybody was greeting each other and letting off fireworks. Happy at last, all our enemies were defeated.

BIFRONS

Bifrons School was divided into boys and girls, and the two never mixed.

Colonel Frank Jenks was headmaster of Bifrons Boys School. He was a disciplinarian of the old school, his idea of running a boys' school was to install a fear of punishment to any boy who disobeyed the rules or got themselves into trouble by any other means. Colonel was his Home Guard rank. One of his favourite methods was to line up, on the stage, any boy that needed discipline, every Monday morning; after recanting to the assembly the alleged misdemeanour, he would make the boy lean over the table, and promptly cane the naughty boy or boys on the back of the thighs in front of the whole school. The other teachers, as far as I have witnessed, only caned the boys on the hand, but there was one who was notorious for accidentally-on-purpose hitting the wrist instead of the hand.

The most disgusting episode I witnessed was on one Monday morning when two twin boys were hauled on stage, Colonel Jenks announced:

'These two boys' mother tells me they were extremely rude to her over the weekend, and refused to do anything she asked them to do'.

He ordered them to lean over the table and began to cane them on the backside quite severely. The boys jumped up and tried to run away. Even though the situation was quite appalling, it was also comical, with the two boys running around the stage and Jenks grabbing them by the hand lashing out trying to hit them. Eventually, the whole school was laughing and to save face Mr Jenks, red-faced, said to the boys that he hoped it would be a lesson to them, and that they were to behave themselves in future.

Mr King took the science class. He was noted for the fact that he had special shaped canes with a hooked end. He kept them soaking in the sink because they stung more when wet. I never knew a session without the canes being used at least once.

Mr Pratt took English and had trouble keeping his class in order. He would rant and rave at the class and as soon as he turned his back to write something on the blackboard someone would call him names; he turned around quickly but could never catch the person doing it. It became so much of a game that, not surprisingly, nobody learnt much.

Mr McCarthy was the geography teacher; a fierce disciplinarian, nobody took liberties with him.

The maths teacher's name I don't recall; perhaps it was because he was such an awful teacher, I quickly put him out of my mind. I do recall that if one didn't follow a lesson it was too bad for you; on with the next. The result was that if one didn't grasp the mathematical concept being taught in the first lesson, you had no chance of understanding the next lesson so one got further and further behind.

The only popular male teacher was Mr Clark; he taught Economics. He was a working-class man's man and could talk one-to-one with us ruffians. If anyone wasn't paying attention in his class, he could throw the blackboard eraser at them with extreme accuracy. He was an out and out communist and most of his lessons were about the Russian 5-year plans.

One day, a couple of slightly inebriated soldiers called into the class; they were old pupils of Mr Clarke. They referred to him as 'Clarkie', which he took in good humour. It turned out they had been members of the 'Chindits' (a British Battalion fighting behind enemy lines in Burma). They were greatly admired in Britain for their exploits in disrupting the Japanese supply and communication network. Colonel Wingate, the battalion Commander, was unfortunately killed in an aircraft crash later. The soldiers tried to get 'Clarkie' to go for a drink with him, but he declined.

The Biology teacher was Miss Metcalf. She was young and pretty; all the boys liked her and delighted in embarrassing her when she came to teaching about sexual reproduction, remembering that no boy at school was over 14 years of age and their only knowledge of sex came from the schoolyard tales. We would press her on in describing, in more detail, how it was possible for a male to fertilise a female and watch in delight as she blushed redder and redder. Poor Miss Metcalf; she was too meek to have been able to survive modern education with boys aged 16 to 17 and next to no discipline.

The other women teacher, I don't recall her name, used to read literature to us. She was a manly kind of woman with cropped hair and used to drive a Singer Sports car. I mainly remember her reading the story of 'Huckleberry Finn,' by Mark Twain, very competently. She had a pleasant mid-country accent and the way she told any story kept us engaged and very quiet for a change.

Apart from the couple of positive memories, last mentioned, I learnt little at that school except how to be streetwise and look after oneself physically; I certainly wasn't educated, but I think education was there for those prepared to knuckle down and accept the discipline.

When I started rebelling against the discipline and the teachers in the schools, I don't know; perhaps it started gradually – unjustly attacked by teachers for defending oneself, being called a 'bully' by bully teachers – the sneering of Mr Comber at Dawson Road School, 'You don't need to bother, Kelly.'

The education at that school was like a three-tier cake: those at the top who were the favourites of the teachers; we never really met them because they never mixed with the mainstream – perhaps we may have seen them when they acted or played in the end of year nativity play. Then the middle layer, the quiet ones who kept their heads down and didn't attract attention. Lastly, the bottom layer, us, who caused the most angst for the teachers; as far as the teachers were concerned, we were dunces. Later in life, most of us were to prove them wrong; it was just their method of teaching, lack of encouragement or leadership, and our rebellion against discipline. Perhaps a psychologist may have a different slant on it.

Fortunately, most of us were avid readers and got a lot of our education from books and newspapers. When I was young, I was forever in the library. Our lack of respect for authority was, in some respect, especially in the Kelly case, learnt from home.

Edwin came to the school after I had left, and he didn't fare any better than I did. Some pupils did all right; incredibly, one of the future Archbishops of Canterbury was a pupil at that school – he attended at about Edwin's time.

Each child was given a third of a pint of milk at morning break. At midday, children were given a subsidised cooked meal for the price of sixpence, which consisted of some meat, mainly mince; Shepard's Pie, or ox tongue, plus two vegetables, or stew. For dessert, it was usually macaroni or rice; if we were lucky, jam tart and custard. One must remember that meat and sugar were in very short supply, and strictly rationed. The idea, of course, was that children in underprivileged areas still got at least one balanced meal per day. Whether that went on all over the country, I don't know.

What did my group do with our sixpence a day and balanced meal?

My small group of friends, forever rebellious, and not the kind willing to knuckle down, had our own idea how this sixpence should be spent. These were the days of aged 13 plus, and the first experiments with smoking. Our clique, of about three or four, would go to the shops at lunch, pool our sixpences and buy a packet of five Woodbine cigarettes (about 5½ pence; a couple of bread rolls each and chips from the fish and chip shop; plus something to drink, then stuff the chips into the roll. All we had to do next was to get a light and smoke a fag each. Then get back to school on time. We used to do that at least two days a week, much to the incredulity of others who would shake their heads in disgust. Our last year at school seemed to be a battle of wits between the teachers and us.

MATCHSTICK ISLAND AND THE DOODLEBUGS

It was an eventful day; I don't remember what day it was, except it was some time in 1944 or 1945. Anyway, it was possibly the heaviest raid by German V1 rockets during that stage of the war. The V1s, some called them 'Buzz Bombs', we called them 'Doodlebugs', started about lunchtime and, as the afternoon progressed, they appeared overhead with increasing frequency. By mid-afternoon, it seemed that there wasn't a moment without one somewhere in the sky; on this day, their motors seemed to be cutting out just over our heads, and we would watch them to see which way they were going to fall. The most frightening moment was when the motor cut out, because the rocket would stall, turn one way or the other, and plunge into the ground with a devastating explosion. The motors had a distinct, fluttering stuttering sound and, when one was flying overhead, everyone would pause in what they were doing and listen for the motor to cut out; if they were inside, people would rush out and try to see which way the flying bomb was heading.

If the flying bomb was heading your way and diving towards you, the only thing to do would be to lay flat on the ground; if possible, behind some mound or shelter. Wherever the 'Buzz Bomb' fell, a pall of smoke would signature its target. Unless one experienced it, it is hard to describe the momentary feeling of terror when one believes the plane is heading straight for you. Looks are deceiving and, fortunately, for us, it landed probably a mile away; although, sometimes it looked as if we were going to be hit by the one-ton bomb. Whatever, someone copped it somewhere. In the entire 'Doodlebug episode', the nearest one to crash near me had hit the ground just over the railway line from our house, about two blocks away. On that occasion, I went straight round after the crash and found the bomb had demolished the front of two houses. In one house, the front wall had peeled away and, strangely, on a table in the living room, stood a glass vase of flowers, untouched. I didn't find out the number of casualties because, by the time I got there, they had been carried away and the police were guarding the scene.

The day of this tale, Jackie Short and I were taking an afternoon off school and, as usual, were spending it on Matchstick Island; a place that featured quite prominently in our lives during the war time years. Whenever school got too boring, or our pending lessons featured Mr. Pratt who took grammar, or Mr. McCarthy who took geography, and it was a nice afternoon, we would play truant, paddle a raft amongst the reeds looking for birds' nests, swim in the deep holes, or just generally enjoy the freedom away from the discipline of school. Pratt and McCarthy were the strictest disciplinarians in the school, apart from Mr. Jenks the Headmaster, who in our eyes was on a par with Adolf Hitler.

How our playground got the name, Matchstick Island, no one knew. Adults we spoke to all came up with various and sometimes far-fetched explanations, but none credible; the name stuck and everyone knew it by that name. It was not even an island, but two large lakes left over from the sand and gravel extracted and used for the building of the Becontree Estate in Dagenham. It was fenced off for safety reasons, as some of the water-filled pits were very deep in places and, pre-war, work had begun to turn it into a boating club; the adjoining Mayesbrook Park was left open for the public. To us children, it was an exciting place: parts of the lake were covered with reeds and bulrushes with nesting waterbirds of all descriptions. In spring and summer, there were frogs and toads and tadpoles to catch, and small fish to angle – mainly minnows and stickleback.

Often in winter, the water would freeze over; except for around the reeds and the deepest parts in the middle, then the lakes were especially dangerous for the unwary. Skating over the ice, avoiding the thinner areas, we would listen carefully for the sound of a crack and, if one was heard, scramble quickly back to the thicker ice. Altogether, it was a magical place: a world of difference from the drab austere days of the war, and the never-ending landscape of houses and streets that surrounded us.

The challenging part for us, though, was that it was forbidden to be there; Park Rangers would keep watch during the day to keep trespassers out, but they were fighting a constant battle to keep us away. In turn, we were always on the lookout for trespassers in our territory, for we had declared it our own property and no other kid was allowed in unless we said so, that is kids of our age or younger.

THE HAIRY GANG

We were the 'Hairy Gang!' How I came to be a member of the gang was simple. One day, I noticed school friends of mine speaking to an older boy and when I approached the bigger boy said to me,

'Who are you? Who said you could hang around here?'

I said, in effect, 'I can go where I liked,' and he said,

'Oh, yeah,' and pushed me.

I pushed him back, and then the usual shuffling and threatening started. I was tall for my age and, in those days, I was very quick to defend myself if threatened. This stranger suddenly stopped, then sniggered and patted me on my shoulder.

'You'll do,' he said, 'I like your style; you can join our gang, provided you pass the 'creeping-in-shop' test'.

'What's the 'creeping-in-shop' test, anyway?' I asked.

'We'll let you know, later,' was the only reply I got.

Until then, my friends had been watching the proceedings with apprehension; now, they were relaxed and all smiles.

'This is Frank,' they said, 'one of our mates.'

The older boy shook hands and said, 'I'm Albert, leader of the Hairy Gang. I liked the way you stood up for yourself.' 'I could have knocked you down any time I liked, but I need tough blokes like you in my gang,' he boasted.

Until then, I didn't know any such gang existed, but decided to go along with it.

I walked along with the group, they congratulated me and told me how brave I was to stand up to Albert. Proud, though I was, I more mystified by it all. I thought he wasn't much of a scare anyway, even though he was older, but they knew him better than I did. It was only later that I found out he had just returned from a stint in Approved School and was on his way to becoming a petty criminal. He associated with the naïve younger boys he was able to dominate and so boost his ego.

Another test required to become a member of the gang, was to learn to swim in Matchstick Island. These lakes were dangerous and we were told several children had drowned in them over the years: some parts were deep and the water cold, so hypothermia could set in quickly. However, we were tough hardy kids, ready for a dare anytime. The gang consisted of up to a dozen local boys belonging to Bifrons School, most of who could swim. I knew how you were supposed to swim but had never really put it into practice. The way we had to learn was, with Albert watching, jump in as far out from the bank as possible, then frantically dog paddle back to shore; it would take your breath away as soon as you hit the icy cold water, even in summer. Soon we could float, swim on our backs, practise the breaststroke and generally enjoy the water.

Someone was always on watch, looking out for the Park Rangers, or 'Parkies' as we called them. As soon as one appeared, depending on how far away he was, we would dress and run or grab our clothes and dress on the run, sometimes with comical results. They could never catch us; we knew the lakes better than anyone, we knew what parts were shallow, what was deep; in our minds, we had a map of submerged pathways and if they came in pairs and tried to cut us off, we would elude them by crossing on one of our secret paths. The best paths were the ones that suddenly shot off, at right angles, to the side of the lake.

On the day of the 'Doodlebugs', Jackie Short and I decided that exploring the reeds of Matchstick Island for birds' nests, and its water for fish life, was infinitely more interesting than struggling with maths and grammar at school. It was one of those balmy summer days: the humming of insects and the sight of the blue sky were more enticing than the drab classrooms. Exploring the shores of the first lake, we became aware of the more than usual activity overhead. By now, after enduring months of attack by this new weapon, we were becoming used to them; however, today seemed to be different. They were coming over more frequently and their motors were cutting out over our heads more often. Luckily, they were all crashing over the rooftops out of our view. Halfway through the afternoon, we noticed one of our dogged adversaries, a Park Ranger, bearing down upon us.

We didn't really want to escape via the lake considering there was only one 'Parkie' chasing us, so we decided to outrun him. During the chase, a couple of the 'Doodlebugs' came over, particularly low, with motors cutting out on approach. We were fearful both times that we might get blown up, but luck was with us again and they carried on gliding away over the rooftops.

This Park Ranger was fit and was gradually gaining on us despite backtracking several times. We were hoping to make it through to the Round House shopping centre before he could get near us; unfortunately, Jackie twisted his ankle and got caught, and the Parkie dragged him off towards the little hut they had at the top end of the park. Jackie was hollering and shouting about his bad ankle, whilst I followed at a discreet distance. They disappeared into the hut for a while and, shortly after, they reappeared; I saw the Parkie let Jackie go, but not before giving him a cuff about the head and a swift kick in the back of his thigh. He hobbled towards me mouthing back at the Parkie that he'd get his father back there shortly to sort him out. The man just yelled at us to get going and not to go back there again, or things would be worse for us. Jackie told me that when they got inside the hut there was a telephone there and the ranger had got on the phone to someone. He was mad and he was scared, whomever he spoke to he said, 'You've got no idea what a terrible time I've had chasing these bloody kids.' 'While I'm chasing these bloody kids, the bloody Doodle Bugs have been chasing me.' Apparently, he was told to give us a warning, and to kick the one he had in the backside before he let him go.

As we walked away, keeping a wary eye out for the Ranger, the excitement died down, and it became noticeable that the 'Doodlebug' activity had also died down; all was peace and quiet again as we made our way home. We laughed and giggled as we went over the eventful afternoon we had gone through; Jackie almost forgot his sprained ankle. We wondered where all those bombs had landed but could only guess it was over towards Barking. There were other things more important on our minds now such as, explaining our day at school and what was to be our excuse to the teacher in the morning.

THE CREEPING-IN-SHOP

The 'Creeping-in-Shop' episode is perhaps one of those instances in life where a crossroads is present before you and it is up to you, and you alone, to decide which route to take.

I was told that I had to pass this 'Creeping-in-Shop' test to become a member of the gang. In summary, all imported goods were in short supply during the war, including cigarettes. Popular brands were the most difficult to obtain. They were sold singularly or in packets if you could get them; often, they were under-the-counter so if the shopkeeper didn't know you, he said he didn't have them. Often a box of loose, unpopular cigarettes was displayed on the counter. Workers on their way home from work, if desperate for a smoke, would buy anything, no questions asked, as long as they were cheaper than the shops. One of the things the gang did was steal cigarettes and then sell them to homeward-bound men as they used the back-alley short cut behind the Roundhouse shops.

In Barking, there was a Tobacconist where the staff was very lax. Our Albert knew these things and had his own mental list of other potential targets. The idea was to walk into the shop casually, and ask for something cheap the gang member knew, in advance, was out the back. When the assistant went out to the back room, the idea was to grab whatever was lying on the counter and run like hell.

On the counter when I went in with the gang member, was a box of at least 150 loose Players cigarettes (a very popular brand). I was now nervous as anything and wondered how I'd got myself into this situation. Did I want to be part of a gang that were just a bunch of petty thieves? At least, I told myself this would be the one and only time I'd be doing it. I just wanted to show these bastards I was as tough as they were, I don't have to continue. Anyhow, when the assistant went into the back room as predicted, I made to take a handful of cigarettes out of the box, my companion mumbled, 'Take the lot.' I did, and we ran away as fast as we could to the rendezvous in Barking Park. In a clump of bushes, a gang of about five of us were laughing and counting out the cigarettes to each other and smoking ourselves silly. The main idea was to keep most of the cigarettes back to sell to workers coming home. I don't know how many cigarettes I smoked that day, or the next, but I know I had a stinking headache. By the time I smoked, and gave away my share, I had none to sell.

Now I could go swimming and rafting on Matchstick Island without being chased off by the Hairy Gang.

I had done my bit; I was now a fully-fledged member of the gang.

Albert and his closest cohorts thought differently, though; their joy in life was stealing, or putting it over other people. He said to me,

'You did all right, Frank; we could use you in a couple of other things I've lined up.'

Not likely, I thought, I'm going to avoid you fellows as much as I can. As mentioned below, I needn't have worried.

To illustrate the mindset of some of my new friends, when I first joined the gang I knew most of the boys, but there were a few that I didn't know. One of the others said to me, that he knew a police officer lived in our house, and that's why he threw a turd at our front window; if he had known I'd lived there, he wouldn't have thrown it.

I recalled the turd in question and remembered it was ignored, as it was slowly taken care of by nature.

I heard them planning other episodes, and I thought: hang on, I don't want to get a criminal record. I made excuses to taking part in any other of their planned escapades. As dad always pointed out to us, that once a person gets a criminal record, they never lose it.

Sure enough, months later, they planned to raid the kiosk in Barking swimming pool one night and the police were waiting. They all got caught. Some who had previous convictions went to approved school; the first offenders got probation. That was the breaking up of that gang.

At the time, I regarded the whole episode as a big adventure, a lark. Without any moralising about the episode, this is what we did and no amount of why's and what's can change it. No doubt, all over Britain gangs of loosely disciplined kids were getting up to similar larks.

STREET URCHINS

These later months of the war, with both parents working, us kids were mainly left to our own devices. Those pre-war days of family outings, bike rides to the forests, were long gone; with Henry and Mildred in the forces, parents working and the pressures of war, they were a distant memory.

Dad, had for some reason, left the police force and was now working as a caretaker for a firm down Silvertown Way that was making precast concrete products. Mum was still working at Briggs Bodies in Dagenham, during the day.

Briggs, along with most other large firms in Britain, used to put on concerts now and again for the workers. I recall once going with Mum to a show that, among others, featured a rising young singer Petula Clark.

In the evenings on midweek-nights, children made up their own games and played in the street: cricket, with a drum for a wicket and a stick for a bat, or a tin can for a football. On particularly cold days, if snow had fallen, we would create an ice slide by walking up and down a strip of road until it became slippery enough to skate on; much to the annoyance of homecoming workers.

Strict times were dictated when to get home. Often, if we were late, mothers would be standing at the gates to give us a clip around the ears as we walked in. Summer was even worse for both mothers and kids; we had double day-light saving time, that meant at the peak of summer the sun didn't set until about ten o'clock so we went further afield, forgetting the time because the sun was so high in the sky. Summer was also the time we spent a lot of time swimming on Matchstick Island and, if the weather were particularly hot, we would go to the Barking swimming pool. Because we rarely had any money to get in, our method was to scale the back wall, which was quite a feat, and sneak in that way. The problem was hiding one's clothes; the attendants were always on the lookout for patrons not using the lockers.

Weekends, apart from breakfast or evening meals, we seemed to spend most of the day walking or cycling somewhere. Generally, the amount of freedom we had was amazing. Apart from our Saturday cinema sometimes, on a Sunday, we'd take a train trip to Upminster, or Hornchurch, and walk down to the Southend Road to watch the cars, seeing who could guess the most makes and models. On the way back to the station, we'd raid someone's apple orchard, stuffing our jumpers with apples. Other times, it was maybe a cabbage or a marrow. No matter, we often came home with some spoil, no questions asked. Our parents didn't care, as long as you weren't caught.

Our father was somewhat ambiguous concerning the law and the policing of it; he gave an implied nod and a wink when it came to stealing a few apples – as long as you weren't caught – but he would be strongly against robbing people, or breaking-and-entering premises. However, when you looked at it, stealing apples was still robbing someone. He would justify it by saying they can afford it.

He was definitely anti-establishment; he couldn't stand the Royal Family or Winston Churchill, whom he termed a war-mongerer). He often related when Winston sent in the troops and police officers on horseback to break up strikes during the Great Depression. He detested any of the so-called upper class – parasites, he would call them – and blamed them, Winston Churchill included, for their part in starting the First and Second World Wars sending hundreds of thousands of young men to their death while staying out of harm's way themselves. He wasn't alone in this thinking though, what I gathered from most of the children I associated with, their parents were of the same opinion.

At the dinner table, Dad would always comment on notable news items and judge them as, either, on someone's incompetence, or that they were on the take. It was amusing at times, but his cynicism of people in authority had the overall effect of turning us into cynics ourselves. A positive slant on this was we were taught not to take everything at face value, but always analyse it first.

Before the outbreak of war, I think he had a sneaky admiration for Adolph Hitler for how he got ahead, despite the fierce opposition from the German ruling class: the story of a working-class man getting the better of the aristocracy. Now that the real horrors of the Nazis were exposed, his admiration turned to the Soviet Union and communism.

Our mother was a different kettle of fish, she was constantly complaining about things; if it wasn't the weather, it would be about the shortages, or the queues at the shops, or anything else she didn't like – not forgetting the kids, especially her own. I think, basically, her problem was having too many children. If she had stopped at three, she may have been happier, but all my life I never knew her to be really happy with us last three; we were constantly being scolded about something. It seemed to me I was particularly picked out for verbal abuse, whether warranted or not, and many a time I was accused of something I hadn't done, but just what she imagined I had. Her choice of weapon for discipline when we were younger was the copper stick; we had an electric Copper for boiling water for washing clothes or for baths. The stick was used to lift the clothes from boiling water. Dad's weapon was his belt. I still recall him running up the stairs undoing his belt on his way to chastise one of the kids.

One way to make extra money was to collect empty soft drink bottles. A shop near the Round House used to pay one penny for each bottle returned. Being the rogues, we were, a ruse was to pinch a couple of the bottles stacked at the back of the shop if the gate was open and redeem them at the front.

Another way was to collect old newspapers and sell them to the fish and chip shop. In those days, the outer wrapping of fish and chips was always of newspaper. We used to go mainly over the Upney side of Maysbrook Park, 'the posh houses,' as we called them). They bought more paper than the working class did. The shop weighed the papers and paid according to the weight. One of our group, thinking to be smart, placed a roof tile inside a bundle of papers. The shop owner was astonished at the weight of the bundle but paid anyway. Unfortunately, that meant we couldn't go back to that shop anymore.

The war was going generally well for the Allies with the German armies on the run, both in Africa and Russia. Britain, and now America, was bombing the German cities relentlessly and we got to know through the media, the names of German cities by the raids upon them; names like Bremen, Dortmund, Hamburg, Frankfurt, the list goes on. Reports were often of 1,000 bomber raids; large industrial areas destroyed. Britain was getting its own back for the destruction caused by the Luftwaffe.

In the Far East, the tide was turning against the Japanese too; the Americans were systemically retaking all the Pacific islands the Japanese had overrun, and were bombing the Japanese mainland. In Burma, New Guinea and Malaya, the British and Commonwealth forces were gaining the upper hand.

During summer holidays, many families would go hop picking in Kent. It was a typically Cockney experience. Most of the families near us went to a town near Maidstone, on the river Medway. I think it was Yalding. Our family never went, but one summer I went with Ronnie Wigget's family for a weekend; I thought it a marvellous experience: a holiday in the country with fresh air, freshly baked bread, and the taste of country food so different from that in London. They lived in a hut beside the hop fields. The kids sometimes helped in the hop fields, but mostly played and fished, and bird nested; the bigger boys chased the girls. After work, the adults went to the local pub for a few pints of beer and a chat, and mums and dads played with the kids. The experience earned them some extra money, which perhaps mainly went on beer, but at least it was a break from the polluted air and routine back in London. Not much joy for the women though, they still had to cook and do the washing, but in more primitive conditions. Perhaps the main reason our mother refused to do it.

DAY AT THE ZOO

We got into trouble with our parents the day when Dennis, Edwin and I were given money to go to the London Zoo. We were streetwise kids so travelling on the Underground, on our own, was no problem; the only problem was discipline amongst ourselves. During the day, at the zoo, Edwin became a real problem, insisting on going back from where we'd been, vanishing from sight every so often. It got so bad, we started to ignore him and let him find us for a change. When it came time for us to go home, he decided he didn't want to go home just yet but wanted to see some more of the animals we saw earlier on in the day. By this time, Dennis and I were tired and wanted to go home and were sick of his antics. We told him firmly we were going now and headed out and for the railway station. He didn't follow. We caught the train to Dagenham and duly arrived home minus Edwin. The first thing Dad asked was where Edwin was. 'We left him at the zoo,' we replied. Dad exploded 'What the hell do you think you were doing leaving him back at Regents Park?' he shouted, 'Where's his ticket?'

'We still have it,' we replied. He frantically put on his bicycle clips, 'He could be anywhere now,' he muttered, and cycled to the local police station to report him missing. Not long after returning home, in walked Edwin as nonchalantly as possible. 'How did you get home?' Dad asked.

'By train,' he replied.

'What about your ticket?'

'Just walked through the barrier,' he just as nonchalantly replied.

PULLING A SWIFTIE

There was the time my bike was stolen, or I thought it had been stolen. The truth never came out all my life, but I think this was a case where I was taken advantage of as I was a child. One morning, I discovered my fairly new bike missing and, in its place, was an older, larger one than mine; it was a lot older, and much shabbier. That weekend, Henry had come home on leave from the army. This was wartime in 1942/3, or there about, and everything was uncertain and in a bit of a mess. What with shortages of food and clothing, transport was also a hit and miss affair. My father was in the auxiliary police at the time and when I announced to him my bike had been stolen, and another one put in its place, he said he would report it stolen and leave the other one at the station to see if anyone comes to claim it. If it wasn't claimed within 14 days, he said, it was mine. The time duly passed and the bike became mine. Mysteriously, my original bike was handed into the police station, according to Dad, who brought it home; coincidentally, my brother was home on leave again. My father said that as I had two bikes, and Henry needed to get to and from the barracks, he could have my newer one because it was more reliable. I wasn't keen on the idea of giving up my new bike and being stuck with the old one, and I said so. Nevertheless, parental authority persuaded me to agree, much to my chagrin. For years, I thought that was the true course of events: that someone had stolen my bike and put an old one in its place. Thinking about it one day, many years later and as I was into middle age, it dawned on me that I had been taken advantage of all those years ago.

THE V2s TO THE END OF THE EUROPEAN WAR

In September 1944, the Germans began launching their V2 rockets. There was no defence against them. The first thing you heard was a loud explosion, followed by the sound of it travelling through the air at the speed of sound. They weighed about 15 tonnes and carried a one-tonne warhead, and they were capable of causing immense damage if landing in the right spot; unfortunately, for the Germans, they were not well guided and landed haphazardly. The nearest one to us landed in Lodge Avenue towards the Robin Hood shops. When I got there on my pushbike, I saw the elderly couple who tended the toilets at Maysbrook Park being carried out on stretchers; the same couple I remembered from when we played there as kids. The front brickwork of the houses opposite had peeled off. One day, I was on a number 62 bus, going to Barking, when a rocket landed just ahead. Ten minutes earlier, and we would have been at the exact spot where it landed.

The era of the V2 rockets was short lived, however, as the armies in Europe and Russia advanced relentlessly against the Germans, and the Royal Air Force pounded the rocket silos and the cities of Germany. I recall once, when out biking with Ron Wigget and Jackie Short riding towards Rainham, we came across a large group of what looked like German prisoners of war on the road, loosely guarded by soldiers; so many, in fact, that we had to get off our bikes to pass through them. The men looked dishevelled, hungry and desperate. To us, it was rather frightening and intimidating. Several asked us for cigarettes and drinks, of which we had none, as we hurried through them. Where they came from, or where they were going, we never found out. Probably due to the rapid advance of the Allies in Europe, and so much of the German army had surrendered, it was better for the British population that German prisoners be returned to the European camps.

The end of the war in Europe was near and people were getting ready for the celebrations. We kids were sent out to gather firewood for a big fire planned in our street. Daily, the newspapers and radio were full of the war and the advances of the Allies, and the uncovering of the grim concentration camps showing the masses of corpses and the emaciated survivors. The German cities were pounded relentlessly, even though their cause was now hopeless. The German population was being punished for starting the war, for the bombing of Britain and for the evils of their leaders, but no doubt, the majority were no guiltier than we were.

When the war in Europe was finally declared over in May 1945, huge celebrations were planned all over Britain. Down our street, on Cannington Road and at the Rugby Road end, a long line of trestle tables was set up in the middle of the road; a piano manhandled out of someone's house and, at the junction to Clementhorp Road, the firewood we had gathered was prepared for the bonfire. The party went on into the night with fireworks, drinking and dancing; some of the adults were getting quite drunk. The part of road where the fire had been got seriously damaged by the heat and, for a couple of years after, a fire was lit there for Guy Fawkes Night, until the council put a stop to it. A few days after the celebrations, when people shook hands, and talked and hugged each other, the adults went back to their usual reserved nature.

***

Children's end-of-war party 1945.
I am at the back, left of picture: dark hair and coat.

Not long after the war's end, all the schools in the Dagenham/Barking area were treated to an afternoon at the cinema. The film shown was a depiction of Shakespeare's 'Henry the Fifth'; each child was given a shiny new three-penny piece on entry. I think the idea was to install patriotism, a feeling of pride in the British race and in the war effort, as in 'Henry the Fifth', despite all obstacles and adversaries, we prevailed and won unconditionally. To my mind, that day was the only day we were treated to a day off by the school, except when evacuated.

The war in the Far East was still raging with huge casualties on both sides, but as history knows, Japan surrendered after the dropping of the atomic bombs. I was in Teignmouth on holiday at that time, as previously said, and joined in the celebrations there. The atrocities by the Japanese, towards their prisoners of war, came to light and that created further hatred of them.

Henry and Mildred came home the same time as each other, and the house was full; particularly, up in the boys' bedroom. Mildred naturally took over her own bedroom, but the five of us had to muck in the other one. Seeing that we only had two beds, it usually went that Henry and Edwin slept in one bed and Pat, Dennis and I slept in the other, head to tail. With Henry there, we really had to behave ourselves; he wouldn't tolerate any mucking about.

By this time, Dad was back at the council doing his decorating job, and Mum had a morning job somewhere in the East End.

November was fast approaching, my 14th birthday and the end of schooling.

There came the careers day when prospective employers came to pick out the boys they wanted for various trades in the factories nearby; mothers came that afternoon to listen for what was on offer. Anytime a prospective boss started to interview me, the headmaster would butt in saying,

'The trouble with Kelly is he won't try.' Consequently, I wasn't offered any job.

Mother said, 'Don't worry about that lot, they only want factory fodder here; I can find you a job.'

A few days later was my 14th birthday, Mother said not to go back to school anymore because she had found me a job at the Co-op butchers at the Round House shops and, seeing I was 14, I could start the next week.

In Britain, the legal smoking age was from 14 years so, at dinner, I calmly brought out a packet of cigarettes and lit up. Dad said gruffly, 'If you keep up that habit, you'll never have any money,' which was hypocritical because he smoked like a chimney.

LIFE IN THE BUTCHERS SHOP

In the 1940s, the word teenager wasn't used; that's an American expression that came into being in the fifties. Young boys and girls were called 'young ladies or men', 'adolescents' or 'youths'; the word ''teenager' hadn't been invented, so you were just a young adult learning to grow up. In some firms, the older workers played tricks on the new starters just to try them out and see how smart they were, but I think one had to be pretty naive to fall for a lot of the tricks. Thankfully, I was working in a shop with only two other workers; the manager, Frank, and another butcher, Harry, who had been brought out of retirement for the duration of the war. Attached to the butcher's shop was the usual grocery and greengrocers' shop, forming the Co-operative, with the grocery manager being in charge overall. Meat, as previously stated, was strictly rationed and in short supply; most of the meat we handled was Australian frozen beef, chilled beef from Argentina and frozen lamb from New Zealand. Only the pork, if any, was home-grown, and home-grown beef or lamb was next to impossible to obtain.

I was to see butchering done the hard way: with axes, cleavers and saws used for dismembering the frozen quarters, and old Harry used to do it with vigour. Always with a cigarette in his mouth, always the same corked tip brand, he had a special knack of flicking out the spent cigarette butt with his tongue so it landed upright on the corked tip. The manager didn't worry if some of the ash landed among the meat, he said no one would be able to taste it anyway. Apart from the rationed meat, the other things sold consisted of off-ration products such as offal, sausages and pies.

Harry was a boxing coach from East Ham way; he was always trying to encourage me to take up boxing.

When I first started, he said, 'Put up your Mitts.'

I did so, and he said, 'Ah, a South Paw.'

'Harry never succeeded in his quest because I didn't see the sense of a sport where you could get a black eye or your teeth knocked out just for the fun of it.

The Round House shops had three butchers, each with their own loyal customers but, when it came to off-rations, it was every woman for herself. Some women seemed to spend most of their time at the shops and knew which shop had what. As soon as a delivery of sausages arrived, as if by a miracle, there would be a queue of women outside the shop. One of the main reasons my mother got me the job at the butchers was that now the family had access to the meat products, which up until now had been very hard to come by; I was now able to bring home the sausages and lambs liver, etc.

Part of my job as butcher's boy was to clean the front entrance each morning, and sometimes there would be a queue forming outside with women standing at the entrance. To move them, I would, in my usual polite way, dash a bucket of water over the front, making the women step smartly away cursing me at the same time.

The floors of butcher shops in those days were covered with sawdust to catch the fat that might be spilled on the floor, and to prevent slipping. You wouldn't want to slip over with a razor-sharp knife in your hand. These days that is considered unhygienic; nevertheless, each day the old sawdust was swept up, and fresh put down every morning.

Monday was generally a slow day, so the manager would parcel up some sausages and perhaps a couple of lamb chops for his mother in Barking, and along with some papers to deliver to the bank, he sent me on the bike to Barking. I remember one day, I returned from Barking and the manager asked me how his mother was. Then I realised, I'd forgotten to drop the meat off at his mother's and had to retrace my journey. In addition, Monday morning was the day I had to render down fat to make dripping, and cook ox tongues; the jobs I hated the most. If rabbits came in, we had to skin them, and when a woman bought a chicken that had to be cleaned. We usually had Monday and Thursday afternoons off, except when a delivery of meat was expected, then the manager would make me stay behind to take delivery.

As well as the passing parade, we had full view of the Round House pub from our shop and saw the SP bookmaker taking bets outside the hotel. Always with a pint of beer at hand and getting fatter and fatter as the years went by.

There were many strikes at that time. The men were slowly being demobbed from the armed forces and returning to civilian life, and they were determined to make conditions better than they were before the war; after all, they reasoned, they fought for six years and won the war and were entitled to better conditions. We at the shop were affected when the transport workers went on strike and the government used troops to deliver the meat. It was comical to see them struggling to handle the big quarters of meat into the shop with the helpful encouragement of the manager.

By now, another butcher, a returned soldier, had started at our shop and poor old Harry had to leave. It was sad to see him go because he was always nice to me.

The first shipment of bananas since before the war arrived in the greengrocer's shop. These were the first bananas anyone had had for six years, so to be fair, the greengrocer manager decided to sell them to customers at the rate of one pound for each ration book. There was talk at the butchers that we had better get in there quick to get our share before they all ran out, so I went in and got my five pound. Unbeknownst to me, my mother came along later and got another five pounds. When the word got out that our family got ten pounds of bananas, it took a long time for me to live that down; especially with the new butcher, who joked I had stolen bananas from a child's mouth.

AUSTERE BRITAIN

The shortage of coal and its delivery to the public became critical just before the advent of winter. When the drivers went on strike, the government arranged for the coal to be dumped in the school playground by army lorry, and everybody had to collect their own coal. It was difficult to carry home, as you can imagine, those owning wheelbarrows became very popular.

England one year after the war was still in poor condition and suffering severe food shortages; it is hard to remember how bleak conditions were with just about everything rationed, services run down, and strikes commonplace. The whole place looked drab and austere. In London, the historic buildings, railway stations and government buildings were black, covered in grime and coal smoke. Even the houses in Dagenham, new before the war, looked drab.

The transport department brought out 'Utility' buses to save money. The main change was the seats were made of wooden slats instead of cushions and were very uncomfortable. The dreariness seems to pass on to the people; most wore black clothes, walked with their hands in their pockets with grim looks on their faces.

Clothing was another item strictly rationed. That, in itself wasn't, of great importance to the young man until he reached the age of about 15–16 when girls suddenly became interesting, then it was time to get measured for his first suit. A suit took about a year's supply of coupons. There was great discussion amongst the lads about who was the best tailor. The one that got the vote from us traded in Barking; he made great pretence about getting over the coupon issue if you had one and promised a quicker job than his competitors. Another issue of course was the money, which parents often helped out with, seeing it was the first suit, and with strict admonishment as that was the last time seeing that you now worked; you paid for all your own clothing in future.

Nevertheless, one never went to town in those days unless neatly dressed.

Radio was still very important to us, as it was during the war; apart from its factual reporting, the BBC put on a lot of comedy shows and dramas. Later, though, offshore 'Pirate Stations' challenged its monopoly; television was still yet to make its reappearance.

Cinema was an important form of escapism for people of that era. Working in the butchers' shop, I got Monday and Thursday afternoon off, and most times that afternoon was spent at one of the local cinemas – especially during the winter, when it was warmer there than at home. Walking down the streets on those afternoons off would sometimes evoke comments from some gossiping women such as, 'layabout', or 'spiv'. Spiv was a term for a man who supposedly lived on his wits and didn't work for a living.

On Sundays, my friends and I usually went to the cinema at Heathway. A friend and I once found a way to get into the cinema for free; we would climb up a drainpipe, adjacent to a window next to the men's toilet, and climb in there. Several weeks later, we spoilt our chances by sitting in the dearer balcony seats. An alert usherette noticed two young lads in the expensive seats, which they obviously couldn't afford, and demanded to see our tickets.

We were well-served by cinemas in those days but, in my opinion, the best one for value was the 'Grenada' on Commercial Road in East Ham. There, not only did you get two films per session, but also between the films, you were entertained for an hour by acts from acrobats to magicians. As you may guess, I have seen practically all the films made in the forties.

It is a funny thing; some people complain about outside influences corrupting the language and culture of one's country. We kids were exposed to a lot of American culture through films and newsreels during and after the war, but none of us picked up an American accent or American ways, though we may have acted out a 'Cowboy and Indian' scenario. Some people cannot get the concept of escapism.

The tensions between mother and me were coming to a climax. I had been working now for almost a year and paying half my wage for board, as expected, and I was of the age when I was beginning to assert my independence as a young adult, but Mum still regarded me as a child and wanted to dominate my life.

The catalyst came when I left my job at the butchers. The end result: I ran away from home.

DARTMOOR

Tramping down the hot bitumen road, weary and footsore, the telephone wires singing their messages down the line, I hear voices among the hums, whistles and shrieks: 'Frank! Frank!' It was my mother's voice, and it was getting louder. Startled and fearful, my pace quickened; I had to get away – she knew where I was, so I had to keep going. I looked around me, up, down and sideways expecting to see her bearing down on me: nothing, just the empty road, the telephone poles with their noisy wires, and the farmer's cows grazing peacefully in the fields.

The sun was getting towards mid-day, and I had eaten nothing since last night. My feet were hurting and few cars had passed me on the road that day; not many people owned cars in 1946, anyway. Those that had passed had not bothered to find out why a 15-year-old boy was walking alone on the road to Dartmoor, and I was thankful for that because I didn't want anyone to know I was running away from home. I didn't want to be found out and taken back.

That was the only time in my life I have heard voices so real and threatening that I actually believed they were directed at me. That was the state of my mind at that time, a mind that was hallucinating, almost bordering on schizophrenia.

It started two days before; well, actually, the build up to it began a week earlier. I was working at the butcher's shop but, lately, I was enjoying it less; particularly since the older butchers were leaving to make room for the ones returning from the forces, and the old happy working life at the shop was no longer the same. The set up at the Co-op was that of the three shops, the grocery manager was the overall boss. There was a new boss out to establish his command and was starting to make life miserable; I was seriously thinking of leaving before that though.

My friend, Jackie, now an apprentice boiler mechanic on the railways, told me he could get me an apprentice job where he worked in Bow. I went for an interview with the supervisor at Jackie's workshop, where he tried me out with a few maths problems. Well, maths has always been my worst subject so as you can guess I didn't shine too well. Jackie assured me I would still get the job anyway because that supervisor had nothing to do with the selection. Therefore, on the strength of that, I filled in the application and next day resigned my job at the butchers. I told my parents, later that day, of my decision. Dad took it okay, but my mother... well, she went berserk, so to speak, and ranted and raved about how she found me that job and how dare I leave it without her permission; her next tirade was about Jackie Short, she yelled,

'You only did it just to work with him; he was always a bad influence. He led you astray,' and that sort of thing; she went on continuously.

The truth, in my mind, was that my parents considered me only bright enough to work at the local butchers, where there were better prospects in obtaining extra meat rations and the like.

She ranted and raved at me continuously so, by nightfall, I was feeling quite ill and my head was spinning. Next morning, to my dismay, she kept at it sending my head into a spin again; I couldn't think straight, my head was so confused. My only wish was that she would go away and leave me alone. I was glad when the time came for her to leave for her part-time job. Her parting words were,

'You go straight back to the butchers today and ask for your job back; I don't want you seeing that Jackie Short again.'

I was used to some form of verbal abuse from my mother, some perhaps warranted, most times not, and ofttimes downright unfair. For some reason, I was not her favourite son, but this tirade was the worst ever.

I had made up my mind: I had to leave home right now before she came back from work. I put on my good clothes, grabbed all the cash I had, my bank book which had about ten pounds in it, and a couple of magazines I was reading at the time and made my way to Becontree Railway Station. On the way, amidst my confusion, I was trying to think of where I was going and the first place that came to mind was Teignmouth in Devon. Though my mind was still ringing with the sound of her voice, my mind was full of happy memories about Teignmouth where I was evacuated just two years previously. In fact, I had never been happy since. That was where I decided to go until... I thought... perhaps I should get a message to them first. In the meantime, I'll go somewhere close.

At Paddington Station, I bought a ticket to Exeter, the Principal City of Devon. The train arrived at Exeter towards evening. I don't remember whether or not I had something to eat, there but I know I took off straight away on foot for the town of Dawlish on the coast; I in my mind, I could still hear her calling me and I was running away in fear. I walked and walked through the night, mainly sticking to paths that ran close to the highway, sometimes having to cross the road, and the heat radiating from the bitumen very noticeable compared to the grassy paths. By dawn, I had reached Dawlish. I decided to skirt Dawlish because I thought people might stop me and ask what I was doing. I was afraid that the word had already got out that I had run away; the feeling that a fugitive criminal must have, avoiding people in case of recognition.

I followed the paths along the cliff tops, dodging a considerable number of tourists on the way, until I was about halfway to Teignmouth. My feet were very painful, I just had to stop to take my shoes and socks off.

I was shocked to discover my feet had formed a number of blisters, which had broken and were now bleeding.

After a rest, I put my shoes and socks on and continued gingerly until I reached the outskirts of Teignmouth. On my walk, I had been trying to sort out in my mind what my next move should be. Now, I reasoned, that my parents would guess I would go to Teignmouth so my next move should be to avoid contacting the Matthews for the time being and get out of Teignmouth without being seen by anyone who might remember me.

I got to the railway station and, luckily, there was a train going to Newton Abbot almost straight away.

Getting out at Newton Abbot, whether or not I got something to eat there I don't recall, I decided to head for Dartmoor; I reasoned that no one would find me there and, if I could get a job, I would survive easily. One of the sporting magazines I had brought from home had a small map of Dartmoor in it and I followed the route shown on it.

It was a hot midsummer's day and with the heat, my lack of food and my weariness no wonder I was starting to hallucinate. I think it was on the road to Buckfastleigh when I thought I heard the voices. Walking on, I noticed up ahead a roadside teahouse advertising Devonshire teas. I decided to rest for a while there and get something to eat, even though I had little cash to spare.

Shortly after leaving the teahouse, the country became hillier and eventually I came to some quite steep hills.

Suddenly, I was in moor country with steepish hills covered in bracken fern and heath with very few trees. By now, it was getting late and the sun was setting; I noticed a gully with a running stream, the banks were covered in blackberry bush and beyond that was a haystack. 'That,' I said to myself, 'is where I'm sleeping tonight.' Therefore, after filling myself with ripe blackberries, I went to the haystack and prepared a bed by teasing out some hay from the bottom of the stack. No sooner had I snuggled into my bed, I was fast asleep.

Next morning, I had a wash in the running brook and a few more blackberries for breakfast before carrying on with my walk. Shortly, thereafter, I came to the village of Poundsgate; a typical old English village with a narrow main road, an old inn and thatched roofed houses. However, the prospects of work didn't look promising, so I kept on walking through. I didn't notice many people about, but I'm sure plenty of people noticed me.

Just beyond Poundsgate, on the left-hand side, a magnificent rugged Tor came into view; I considered it high enough to climb and view the surrounding countryside.

It was a nice view from the top as the extent of the moor could be seen. Looking down on the roadside, I noticed a small farmlet with cows grazing, and heard a woman's voice and a dog barking; I imagined she was calling the cows in for milking. Except for the isolated farm, the surrounding countryside was just moorland for as far as the eye could see.

After some time up there, where I rested and read some of my magazine, I descended back to the road and continued on my journey. While up on the mountain, I was pondering my next move: my mind was settled now and the reality of my situation was becoming clearer. Where the farmlet was, there was a junction in the road; the road straight ahead went to a village called Dartmeet and onwards to the north of Devon; to the right, it led to a village called Pondsworthy and on to Widcombe-in-the-Moor made famous from the song, 'Old Uncle Tom Cobbly and all'.

I should continue, I said to myself, through to the North Coast of Devon, avoiding the town of Princetown, the location of the infamous Dartmoor prison.

When I reached the farm, the woman was standing on the road. Going to pass her, I was taken completely by surprise when she said, 'Please can you help my uncle get in the harvest?' She was a woman in her mid to late thirties, pretty and a bit plump. 'I can give you a good feed.'

Taken aback, I stammered, 'I don't know.'

'Please,' she said, 'he is an old man and is doing it all on his own.'

My mind was racing; I hadn't had a decent meal for days and this was a good opportunity to eat and take a rest from walking. 'Okay,' I said.

Her eyes lit up, 'Oh, thanks; I'll go and introduce you to my uncle Fred. My name's Mary, by the way'.

She led me to a field off the road where Fred was sitting down sharpening a scythe with a whetstone. It was a field of oats, and I could see about a third of it had been cut by scythe – the cut oats lying down in neat rows.

Fred was a spritely fit man of 74 years. After being introduced, he said he wanted me to gather the cut oats in armfuls, starting on the dry oats, and tie them together using some of the oat straw. He demonstrated how to do it and then, with the scythe, promptly carried on cutting the oats at a steady rhythmic pace, laying it down in neat rows; making it look so easy.

About mid-day, Mary arrived with a basket full of sandwiches and a jug of cold cordial and we sat down to lunch. They didn't pry too much into my circumstances or where I was going, but mainly talked about how late they were with the harvest and all the work that needed to be done before the onset of winter; they were only too pleased to have a helping hand.

The oats we were gathering were winter feed for the cattle, and then there was bedding to be gathered to house them. The winters in this part of the moors can be very severe and snowfalls can sometimes cut the farm off for days.

After lunch, Fred jumped up and said he would go and fetch the horse and cart so we could begin carting in some of the oats.

We loaded up the cart to the limit and took it back to unload and stack the oats in the barn. As usual at these farms, there was a wide space between the farmhouse and the barn where the manure from the barn was stacked, and in spring the manure was carted out to be spread on the fields. Manoeuvring the cart backwards to the barn entrance involves a lot of cussing and yelling from the farmer as the carthorse struggled with the load.

When the first load was finally unloaded and the horse separated from the cart, it was back to the field for a bit more work before the evening meal.

It was a large meal, as Mary had promised. After we had eaten, Mary asked me how long I could stay and, if possible, at least until all the oats were in because there was still plenty of work for me if I wanted it.

'About a week,' she hinted.

Secretly, I couldn't believe my luck. 'Okay,' I replied, 'I'm in no hurry to go north; as long as I'm there before winter.'

Picture of farmhouse taken about 1995

The farm kept chickens and a few ducks, as well as the handful of cows. Fred had his own riding mare he used for shopping, tobacco and such, and socialising. Mary sold some of the milk, butter and eggs and any surplus vegetables at the local village, and to the infrequent passing traffic.

Once a week, a delivery lorry called at the farm, selling meat, groceries and other necessities.

The farmhouse itself was very old; perhaps pre-18th century, as it had a heavily thatched roof and water was obtained using a hand pump connected to an underground spring. Everything was done by hand at this place and it seemed like it was a constant battle to make ends meet.

Early next morning, straight after breakfast, we went back to the field. I continued bundling up sheafs of oats, whilst Fred methodically cut down the oats, swaying side to side with the scythe – step-by-step, as he progressed down the row – only stopping now and again to get out the whetstone to hone the blade.

After lunch, Fred said we would start carting more oats back to the barn and left to harness up the carthorse, while I continued standing up the sheafs. He told me there was lots of work to be done before winter set in because, once it snowed up here, the farm could become isolated. After the oats, there was the winter bedding to be cut and brought in, and the potatoes to dig up and store he said, 'Though the weather was fine and hot at present, it can change suddenly.'

To emphasise the urgency of getting the oats in, he loaded the cart up as high as we could reach with the pitchfork. Reaching the barn, I climbed on top of the load with my pitchfork, while Fred backed the horse in.

Then, all of a sudden, it seemed that the world had turned upside down; I found myself falling to the ground along with the load of oats and the pitchfork too. Luckily, I survived the tumble unharmed and scrambled out to find Fred struggling with the frightened horse. It turned out that the shaft broke under the strain of the overloaded cart.

Disaster: the only place where the shaft could be repaired was in Poundsgate, and the repair would take several days; the only other way to bring in the oats, meanwhile, was by the snow sled. Therefore, while the shaft was repaired, we continued bringing in the oats by sled. That also meant Mary had to ask me to stay a bit longer than originally agreed to. By now, I was getting quite used to the good food and comfortable bed, so I said I would stay as long as they needed me, for which they were very grateful.

The sled only carried about an eighth the quantity of the hay cart; it was slow, twice as much work, but necessary. Gradually, we wore down the field of oats and by the time the shaft was repaired, we were reaching the last of the oats.

With the cart back in use, we soon had the rest of the oats in then started gathering bracken fern from the moor for the cows bedding.

When the winter weather really sets in, the fields are covered in snow and the cattle have to be housed in the barn, this necessitates fresh bedding every day. Each morning, after the milking, the bedding and the manure had to be cleaned out and stacked outside to be spread on the fields in spring. Most farms use straw, this one used fern. The oats were a good supplementary winter feed, both for the cows and the poultry, the main feed being hay. Next, there were the potatoes to dig up and store, the nights were getting very cold now and the rush was on before the ground got too cold. The potatoes were ploughed up and Fred's method of storing them was to dig a trench alongside the hedgerow, lay down a thick layer of fern and, on top of that, several layers of potatoes; cover them with more fern and top it off with the dirt dug out from the trench.

I was beginning to enjoy my life on the farm; the outside work had strengthened me up a lot and my skin became well-tanned. Fred had found me an old pair of boots to work in because my old shoes were just about falling to pieces. Mary gave me an old coat of her fathers. The coat was of a blue colour with a cut-away front. It immediately reminded me of the 17th century pirates in 'Treasure Island', the book by Robert Lewis Stevenson; the illustrations in which showed such style of coat. It made me feel like a modern-day buccaneer.

For perhaps the first time in my life, I was treated like an adult and the feeling was great. I was feeling quite at home. No mention was made of when I was leaving and, secretly, I was a bit apprehensive about my future after the farm, but at no time did I consider returning home.

Fred smoked a pipe and enjoyed a smoke in the evening; he gave me one of his old ones to keep him company. Mary had made some elderberry wine during the summer and we enjoyed a glass of that now and again. Once a week, Fred and I would walk to Pondsworthy, where he had friends, to buy his stock of tobacco; he advised me to stay outside in case people asked questions.

Fred was generally a happy soul and when in a singing mood, the only songs he knew were hymns, which he sang at the top of his voice. He and Mary were completely unsophisticated with little knowledge of life outside their area; he showed me a torch that he couldn't get to work, and I discovered the batteries weren't making contact and bent the tabs over so they touched. He was amazed to see the torch working and asked me if I could fix his radio. I laughed and told him that was too complicated for me. Mary strongly believed in witchcraft and spells. Any day, when the cows were being contrary and difficult to bring in for milking, she would say someone must have put a spell on them. When I laughed and said, 'It was rubbish,' she became quite concerned. 'Don't say that' she said, 'you'll make it worse.' Later, she showed me a crystal ball she had bought from a travelling Gypsy; these Gypsies prey on superstitious people who they coerce into buying things they don't need or want.

Soon it was time for the Widecombe Fair, very famous in the district and a big event for the locals where the people gathered to show off their wares or to socialise with old friends. We went by horse and cart and while there, I decided to withdraw some money from my savings account to spend at the fair. For Mary and Fred, it was one of the big events of the year though I found it fairly tame.

The local vicar came around once and gave me a few quizzical looks. He asked me where I came from, but I just said I wasn't from Devon, which was fairly obvious.

My 16th birthday was coming up, when I told Mary my age, she didn't believe me, but said she would buy me something at Tavistock where she and other locals always go just before Christmas.

When my 16th birthday arrived, she presented me with a new pair of boots; proper farming boots with high waterproof uppers to keep the mud and water out, sorely needed at the time I must say. All my life, I have always fondly remembered what I had for my 16th.

Mary was getting quite friendly with me by now and enjoyed a hug and a cuddle. I found out that after her father died, she was left to run the farm on her own with a hired hand. This hired hand was a local; after a while, he began making advances towards her, which she rejected. He became aggressive and the climax came when he tried to force himself on her and she ran to the house and locked herself in. He ran around the house naked trying to find a way in but gave up after a while. That is when her uncle Fred moved in to work the farm.

The first touch of winter arrived with bitter cold nights, sleet showers and a sprinkling of snow; it was nice to huddle together around the fire with a sip of elderberry wine and a pipe full of tobacco. Fred and I slept upstairs and Mary down below. She would sometimes call up, 'My bed's nice and warm, Frank; why don't you come down?' Fred would give me a nudge, I was worried though because any time we got friendly she would always say, 'You will marry me if I get pregnant, won't you, Frank?' I worried because first, I definitely didn't want to get married at 16, and second, she was more than twice my age.

Fred had a 'lady friend' at Dartmeet and, once a week, he would get dressed up, saddle his mare and take off to visit her. I would try to vanish somewhere, such as walking or climbing the Tor, while all the time Mary would be looking for me and calling out.

The first heavy fall of snow occurred, covering the whole countryside in a thick blanket. In the morning, I went out as usual to let out the chickens, they made quite a fuss trying to avoid jumping onto the snow; I was laughing at their antics when, out of the blue I heard, 'Frank!'

My heart gave a jump. Standing at the gate was Dad; rugged up, face pinched with cold. The dog rushed barking to him, I called her back. 'What are you doing here?' I blurted out, more in astonishment than questioning.

'I've come to take you home,' he said.

'How did you find me?'

'Oh, you know, it's like a game of chess; you make a move and we make a move,' was all he would say.

He wouldn't elaborate any further, but my mind flashed back to the day at Widecombe Fair when I withdrew money from my savings account and the vicar's questions before that.

I said I didn't want to go home, and he said he could make me go because I was underage, but wanted me to come of my own accord. I said that I understood that when a person reached 16 years of age, he could choose for himself. Dad said that was not so. I was a bit confused because his sudden appearance had thrown me. He said they all missed me, but I replied that all they missed was my money, but that I didn't run away because of him, it was because of Mum. He nodded and said he knew. By this time, Mary had come out. I introduced her and they had a short conversation. I didn't quite hear all they said, but I did hear him say something about wages. I butted in to say I had everything I wanted.

He then said, 'I'm going back to the hotel at Poundsgate now and will come back to pick you up this afternoon. I've booked your ticket on the bus to London'.

We went back into the farmhouse a bit shocked and uncertain what to do. One thing for sure, they knew back home where I was now. After some discussion, not knowing the law well enough about where I stood, I reluctantly decided I had to go back home. Mary was upset about it but agreed it was the only option. She gave me two pounds from her small savings for the trip. Late that afternoon, Dad picked me up as planned and we stayed the night in the hotel. Next morning, we got to Newton Abbot to catch the bus. At the terminal, Dad said, 'You'd better buy your ticket for the journey.'

I remember him saying, yesterday, he had paid for my ticket and now he was lying already.

After a long and tiring journey, we arrived in London and got the electric to Becontree. My long adventure was over and now back to the modern life and the drab surrounds of Dagenham.

My brothers, who were keen to hear of my adventures, eagerly greeted me upon my arrival. The evening meal was a more sober affair; Mum sniffed and said, 'You should have told us where you were', but with a stern glance from Dad, nothing more was said.

My friends were more interested to hear my tales, but Lorrie Rainer, who was always inclined to exaggerate, said, 'Gee, I thought you had stowed away on a boat and went to China.'

All through the centuries, songs were sung and tales were told of a mother's love and the special bond between mother and son; in our case, it was bordering on a case of mutual dislike.

Jumping forward to 1978, and the last time I saw our mother – I had spent the last 18 years in Australia, mainly working outdoors in the hot Australian sun, so I was quite tanned – she looked at me with a mixture of embarrassment and distaste, 'Why are you so dark?' she asked, 'you look like a Dago.'

GRIMY LONDON

The normal November fogs were denser now than they had ever been the result of increased motor traffic and the corresponding higher use of coal fires. Each year, they got progressively worse so that by the late forties, they got so bad that on the worse occasions, motorists couldn't see the kerb to find their way home, and so abandoned their vehicles.

At Dagenham, I saw Boy Scouts leading buses back to the depot by shining torches on the kerb in front for the driver to follow; at East Ham, on the busy cross road of Barking Road and East Ham High Road, large gas fired flares were used in an attempt to burn up the fog.

I recall one evening, a friend and I were walking home from the Round House shops and, due to the very thick fog, became disoriented; we couldn't see the houses across the street and couldn't work out what street we were in, and so knocked on the door of one of the houses to find out. To our surprise, it turned out to be Cannington Road.

One could not walk the street without getting a layer of dirty black soot sticking to your eyebrows. I believe in one night alone, over a thousand elderly people died from respiratory failure. The authorities were forced to act and eventually banned the use of household coal fires.

In our house, in the late 1940s, everyone smoked; if all were at home, for one reason or another, there would be about eight people sat around the table smoking and a pall of smoke drifted up to the ceiling. If you add to that, the fog and the general atmospheric pollution about London, it's a wonder any of our lungs survived past thirty years of age. Dad had a theory then that smoking couldn't harm you because the lungs were being constantly washed with phlegm; a theory being disproved then and definitely disproved now.

My situation now, after the Dartmoor episode, was to get a job as soon as possible, which I got early the following week as a delivery boy for a one-man bakery in Ilford. The baker did all the work by himself from running the ovens, making the dough and baking the bread and buns. Attached was a shop, which was run by his wife. My job was to deliver bread to the customers by way of a two-wheeled bike, which had a large box affair as a sidecar to carry the loaves. Put together by the baker himself, the tricycle was a monster of a thing to propel and was always threatening to fall apart; in addition, I was forever ripping holes in my pants from the springs poking through the saddle.

In theory, the job was to deliver loaves of bread, but in fact, most mornings when I arrived at work on the appointed time, the dough still hadn't been put in the ovens so I had to wait until they were baked and then assist in knocking out the bread before I could load my sidecar. At my age, just 16, I didn't consider all the hard work the baker did.

The only thing I liked about the job was eating one of the steaming half loaves of wholemeal bread while on my deliveries. I decided, after a few weeks, that this job wasn't for me and resigned.

The first couple of years after the war were very popular for weddings as people returning from the forces were making up for lost time.

Henry was now courting Rose Alfreds, the girl next door; they decided to get married and the wedding was in June 1946.

Weddings weren't lavish affairs in the 1940s, even if you could afford it, because everything was in short supply. Fortunately, for them, Kenneth, Rose's brother, worked for British Airways on the UK-New York route and was able to sneak in a few bottles of scotch and other scarce-to-get items. The up result was that everyone could get a lot to drink, if not much else. Dad got drunk for the first time since swearing off drink, during the war, when he hit the bottle at the concreting works and Mum had to go and collect him.

There was a posh restaurant on Barking Road where Rose wanted the reception, but I think only the meal was held there as it was booked out, so the reception was held at our house. All had a good time and the main thing was it was a release from the tense austerity of the times.

In 1947, the following year, Mildred got married to Alfred Sindall, a long distant Lorry Driver – he was a pleasant man and liked by everyone. Again, the reception was at our house. However, there was not as much drink as at Henry's wedding, but still all had a good time.

One year during my holidays, I went with Alf on one of his long distant trips. At the time, he was working for a firm in Barking, delivering tiled fireplaces to towns all over the north of England. This trip was to Nottingham and various places in between. We stayed the night in lodgings in Nottingham. The sleeping quarters were a large dormitory sleeping about ten men; I made a fool of myself by drinking too much beer and being sick all over the dormitory floor. I think I was about 17 at the time.

HAINS AND WARWICK

My next job lasted me until I was called up for National Service in the army; this job was for a firm called Haines and Warwick. They were real estate property managers for a considerable part of East London; their home base was in Seven Kings. Apart from collecting rents, they were responsible for carrying out repair work to the buildings.

I was employed as a labourer for one of their jobbing tradesmen. I found Fred, the tradesman, working in Gwendolyn Avenue, Plaistow; he was installing a new fireplace in one of the rented properties. After introductions, I did the various tasks I was instructed to do, then we went to Plaistow were the depot was based – near the railway station.

As anyone who knew this area in the forties, it was a fairly grim sort of a place with narrow streets, some cobbled; houses built of discoloured London brick with slate roofs and with tiny front and back gardens. I don't know how old the houses were, but the scenario put me in mind of a Dickensian set as might be depicted in an old black and white movie. At this depot, each day, we would load up a large steel-tyred cart with all the materials needed for the jobs we were doing. As some of our work was repairing leaking roofs, on top of the cart, an extension ladder and a duckboard were tied for climbing over the roof. We would then depart, pushing the fully loaded cart, steering by way of the duckboard, to the various properties. Sometimes, the work destination was too far away to complete in one day, such as at the Barking end of East Ham. On the way, Fred would perhaps do a couple of small jobs and, when we got to the destination, leave the cart in the front garden of the property for the night and find our way back to the depot.

Each week, the foreman would arrive at where we were working, check our progress, find out what supplies were needed, and give Fred another pile of work orders. Fred was a competent tradesman, skilled in most aspects of the building trade, and even though we had a somewhat fiery relationship at times, I learnt a lot of building techniques from him, which I never forgot. The skills I picked up came very useful in later life.

Just imagine pushing that cart through the East End streets among the traffic. The side roads were all right, but when we came across a busy main road, or perhaps travelled along a short way with the buses, it got especially difficult. Some goods were still delivered by horse and cart and, when they came into view, we had to stop and let then pass so as not to frighten the horse. Unbelievably, brewery drays were still used to deliver beer to the pubs around Plaistow, in the late forties. They made such a racket rattling over the cobbled stone roads; they showed off the strength of these horses and indeed the danger of these vehicles. These days, of course, it would be impossible to push a cart through all the traffic, or to use a horse.

These cobble-stoned streets also made it hard to steer our cart; the steel tyres caused the cart to bounce all over the place. Some of the steeper railway bridges took some pushing to get over, this caused quite a few clashes between Fred and me. Because of the long ladder and duckboards that projected beyond the cart handle, it was difficult to steer and push at the best of times. When the pushing became a bit of a struggle, I would look over to Fred and see he only had one hand on the cart.

'You pushing, Fred?'

'Course I am.'

'No, you're not; I've got all the weight.'

So would begin another fiery argument.

Fred was an ex-serviceman and served in the North Africa campaign and in Italy. I don't know what part he played in the war, but like a lot of ex-service men of that period, he had quite a chip on his shoulder, so it was easy to get him started. He was always warning me on how I would cop it in the army once I was called up and bemoaning that he had fought in the war just to save the country for the likes of me.

The nature of the work kept us extremely fit; after all, unless you were fit, you couldn't do the work, that fitness kept me in good condition for my stint in the army when I was called up for National Service.

I recall one period in the army when I was in Didcot; the commanding officer put the whole battalion through the obstacle course. The Major in charge, we called him the Mad Major – I think every battalion had a Mad Major – was disgusted by the unfitness of some of the troops; he decided that we all had to go through it again. At that time, I was in the battalion rugby team and so was the Major, and I knew how fearless he was.

He declared, 'There are only two men in this company that went through the course properly: Kelly and Patterson.' Patterson, a boxer, was very fit too.

'These two men are going to go through it again, first, to show you lot how it is done properly.'

'When you lot go through it again, I expect you also to do it properly.'

Though we didn't really want to go through it again, we had to; we did so with no problem and the Major was satisfied.

The large part of our work was for leaking roofs and most of the houses were terraces with badly built back-additions; this, generally, meant we had to pass through the houses to get to the back. Broken tiles did not cause all the leaks; many were caused by the failure of the flashing around chimneys and dividing walls. We always had to carry zinc sheet, plus sand and cement with us too. While the majority of houses were quite clean, a tiny handful was notoriously dirty and vile smelling. We always dreaded going to those places. One or two made us gag as soon as we entered the door; you had to hold ones breathe as we walked through the house to the back. If the occupier offered a cup of tea during the day, you would quickly refuse but if it were too late, we would pour it away as soon as possible without the tenant seeing you.

The worse smelling house was in Stratford and I swear that if a search were made, a dead body would have been found. The stench was awful.

The firm also had contracts for repair work in a chain of groceries. These shops were called 'Green Stores' and were distinguished by having bottle-green tiles on the front facades. These were good days for us; they gave us a respite from trudging through the streets of London pushing that cart. We travelled to shops as far away as Southend and Billericay, doing minor repairs and replacing many of those green tiles.

Another job we did was at the Whitbread Brewery repairing concrete floors. At lunchtime, the brewery opened up a caged affair filled with various brands of their brew for the workers to have a free drink with their lunch; we were always first at the beer enclosure lunchtime to pick out our favourite beer, much to the annoyance of the regular brewery workers.

Sure enough, in late 1949, soon after I turned 18, my call up notice arrived. I remained in that job right up until I had to report to the RAOC training depot in Aldershot.

EPILOGUE

We have come to the end of my recollections of the various ups and down in our family in the 1930s and 40s. Naturally, it is mainly centred on me, but I hope it gives an insight of how one's upbringing and environment may determine the future decisions of an individual and mould his character. I could have added a lot more to it, but I think I have given an outline of what things were like. I hope you enjoy it.

I believe the dramatic events, the setbacks, and forced separations we experienced as children played a good part in giving us greater resilience in adult life in times of disappointments or adversity. Those that weren't able to learn this lesson have struggles.

The children of the 30s and 40s, with all their good and bad points, were now adults.

While the rest of the family were settled by now, in their various occupations, Edwin and I were far from settled. I believe we were the result of poor schooling and lack of discipline. We had the intelligence, but at that time didn't know how to put it to good use. In the end, the future was to prove that we did all right.

In hindsight, our parents had a difficult time raising a family of six on limited income, starting with the Great Depression then going almost straight away into the deprivations of another world war. Mum couldn't cope with a large family and I think she resented the last three of us; that may be why she was such a grump. Dad, I think, was proud of his family, and did his best to install a sense of pride in ourselves. Henry and Rose, as with Mildred and Alf, had children by now.

My future is another story. The advantage in not having a trade, meant I was able to earn my living from various occupations later on, with many adventures along the way; occupations such as soldier, merchant seaman, butcher, shooter, tunnel worker, road worker, demolitions expert and, lastly, a railway worker for the New South Wales railways.

Obviously, the world today is a vastly different place to the 1930s and 40s, and though the changes have been accelerating since then at an ever-faster rate, the people are the same.

Let us hope the politicians and educators don't neglect history; hopefully, they will learn from it.

www.ingramcontent.com/pod-product-compliance
Lightning Source LLC
LaVergne TN
LVHW021952060526
838201LV00049B/1675